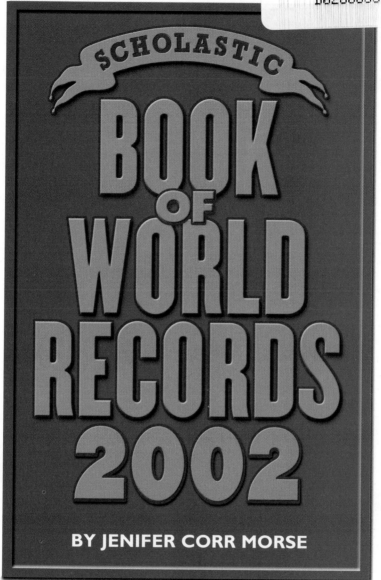

# SCHOLASTIC
# BOOK OF WORLD RECORDS 2002

## BY JENIFER CORR MORSE

A GEORGIAN BAY BOOK

SCHOLASTIC
REFERENCE

To Bill and Rose Corr—the world's greatest parents.
–Jenifer Corr Morse

CREATED AND PRODUCED BY GEORGIAN BAY ASSOCIATES, LLC

©2001 by Georgian Bay Associates, LLC
All rights reserved. Published by Scholastic Inc.

**Georgian Bay Staff**
Bruce S. Glassman, Executive Editor
Emily Kucharczyk, Photo Editor
Barbara Wertel, Fact Checker

**Scholastic Reference Staff**
Kenneth R. Wright, Editorial Director
Mary Varilla Jones, Editor
Elysa Jacobs, Editorial Assistant
Nancy Sabato, Art Director

**Cover Photo Credits**
Cover photographs courtesy Photodisc

In most cases, the graphs in this book represent the top five record holders in each category. However, in some graphs, we have chosen to list well-known or common people, places, animals, or things that will help you better understand how extraordinary the record holder is. These may not be the top five in the category. Additionally, some graphs have fewer than five entries because so few people or objects reflect the necessary criteria.

ISBN 0-439-31398-8

10 9 8 7 6 5 4 3        02 03 04 05
Printed in the U.S.A.   23
First printing, November 2001

# Contents

## Money and Business Records 193

## Sports Records 211

## Popular Culture Records 276

# Nature
# Records

**Animals • Disasters • Food
Natural Formations • Plants • Weather**

# World's
# Fastest Flyer

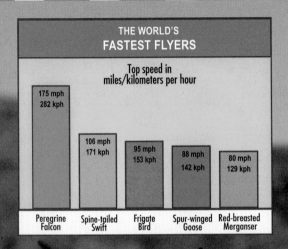

THE WORLD'S
**FASTEST FLYERS**

Top speed in
miles/kilometers per hour

| Peregrine Falcon | Spine-tailed Swift | Frigate Bird | Spur-winged Goose | Red-breasted Merganser |
|---|---|---|---|---|
| 175 mph 282 kph | 106 mph 171 kph | 95 mph 153 kph | 88 mph 142 kph | 80 mph 129 kph |

# Peregrine Falcon

When diving through the air, a peregrine falcon can reach speeds of up to 175 miles (282 km) an hour. That's about the same speed as the fastest race car in the Indianapolis 500. These powerful birds can catch prey in midair and kill it instantly with their sharp claws. Peregrine falcons range from about 13 to 19 inches (33 to 48 cm) long. These birds of prey live in both the open country and the bustling city. In fact, New York City is home to the largest concentration of peregrine falcons anywhere in the world.

# World's Largest
# Bird Wingspan

# Marabou Stork

This large bird has a wingspan that can reach up to 13 feet (4 m). Marabou storks weigh up to 20 pounds (9 kg) and can grow up to 5 feet (150 cm) tall. Their long leg and toe bones are actually hollow. This adaptation is very important for flight because the bird is lighter. Although marabous eat insects, small mammals, and fish, the majority of their food is carrion—already dead meat. Since these storks need to eat about 1.5 pounds (700 g) of food a day, this makes them an important part of nature's clean-up crew.

### THE WORLD'S LARGEST BIRD WINGSPANS
**Wingspan in feet/meters**

| Marabou Stork | Albatross | Trumpeter Swan | Mute Swan | Whooper Swan |
|---|---|---|---|---|
| 13 ft. 4 m. | 12 ft. 3.7 m. | 11 ft. 3.4 m. | 10 ft. 3 m. | 10 ft. 3.1 m. |

# World's Heaviest
# Flighted Bird

## Great Bustard

Male great bustards can measure up to 4 feet (1.2 m) long and weigh up to 40 pounds (18 kg). They also have wingspans that can measure about 8 feet (2.4 m) in width. Males are usually about four times larger than females. These birds use their large, powerful wings to take off and sustain flight. Bustards have long legs and only three toes. When they are frightened, these birds are capable of running very fast. Great bustards mostly inhabit the grassy fields and prairies of southern Europe and central Asia.

### THE WORLD'S HEAVIEST FLIGHTED BIRDS

Weight in pounds/kilograms

| Great Bustard | Trumpeter Swan | Mute Swan | Albatross | Whooper Swan |
|---|---|---|---|---|
| 40 lb. 18 kg. | 37 lb. 17 kg. | 36 lb. 16 kg. | 34 lb. 15 kg. | 34 lb. 15 kg. |

# World's Largest
# Flightless Bird

## Ostrich

An ostrich can grow up to 8 feet (2.4 m) tall and weigh up to 300 pounds (136 kg). These African birds lay giant eggs, averaging 3 pounds (1.4 kg) each. The volume of just one of these eggs is equal to two dozen chicken eggs. Ostriches can run at speeds of up to 50 miles (80.5 km) per hour. With their long legs, they can cover 15 feet (4.6 m) in a single bound. Ostriches also use their powerful legs to kick at enemies, and some have even been known to kill lions.

### THE WORLD'S
### LARGEST FLIGHTLESS BIRDS

**Height in inches/centimeters**

| Ostrich | Emu | Cassowary | Rhea | Emperor Penguin |
|---------|-----|-----------|------|-----------------|
| 96 in. 243.8 cm. | 60 in. 152.4 cm. | 60 in. 152.4 cm. | 54 in. 137.2 cm. | 45 in. 114 cm. |

# World's Smallest Bird

# Bee Hummingbird

The male bee hummingbird measures barely 2.5 inches (6.3 cm) from the tip of its bill to the end of its tail. In fact, its tail and bill alone make up one-half of the bird's length, which is about equal to the width of a baseball card. These tiny flying creatures are found in Cuba and on the Isle of Pines in the South Pacific. Like most other hummingbirds, they are able to fly forward, backward, and straight up and down. They also have the unique ability to hover in midair. Bee hummingbirds, which weigh only about .07 ounce (2 g), are also able to beat their wings at speeds of up to 80 times per second.

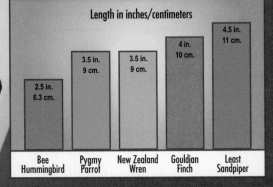

THE WORLD'S
SMALLEST BIRDS

Length in inches/centimeters

| Bee Hummingbird | Pygmy Parrot | New Zealand Wren | Gouldian Finch | Least Sandpiper |
|---|---|---|---|---|
| 2.5 in. 6.3 cm. | 3.5 in. 9 cm. | 3.5 in. 9 cm. | 4 in. 10 cm. | 4.5 in. 11 cm. |

# World's Longest-Lived Bird

## Andean Condor

Andean condors, members of the vulture family, can live to be 70 years old. That is almost as long as a human's life span. Andean condors are some of the largest flying birds, measuring more than 4 feet (130 cm) long and weighing about 24 pounds (11 kg). They also have a wingspan of more than 10 feet (3 m). These birds are found from the Pacific coast of South America to the Andes Mountains. Although they are birds of prey, Andean condors are mostly scavengers and prefer to eat carrion.

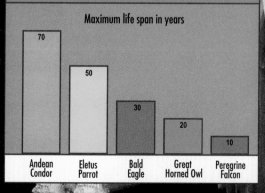

THE WORLD'S
**LONGEST-LIVED BIRDS**

Maximum life span in years

| Andean Condor | Eletus Parrot | Bald Eagle | Great Horned Owl | Peregrine Falcon |
|---|---|---|---|---|
| 70 | 50 | 30 | 20 | 10 |

# World's Smallest Fish

# Dwarf Pygmy Goby

Measuring only .5 inch (13 mm) long at the most, the dwarf pygmy goby is the world's smallest fish. It is also one of the smallest living animals with a backbone. Unlike most gobies, this species lives in freshwater, and can be found mainly in the Philippines. These fish must, however, return to saltwater to breed and hatch their eggs. Gobies usually lay only a few eggs at a time and sometimes care briefly for their young, which are called ipon.

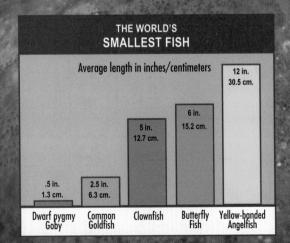

### THE WORLD'S SMALLEST FISH

Average length in inches/centimeters

| Dwarf pygmy Goby | Common Goldfish | Clownfish | Butterfly Fish | Yellow-banded Angelfish |
|---|---|---|---|---|
| .5 in. 1.3 cm. | 2.5 in. 6.3 cm. | 5 in. 12.7 cm. | 6 in. 15.2 cm. | 12 in. 30.5 cm. |

# World's
# Biggest Fish

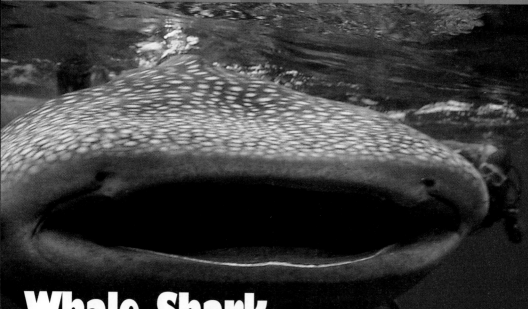

# Whale Shark

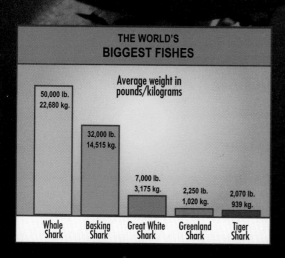

**THE WORLD'S BIGGEST FISHES**

Average weight in pounds/kilograms

| | | | | |
|---|---|---|---|---|
| 50,000 lb. 22,680 kg. | 32,000 lb. 14,515 kg. | 7,000 lb. 3,175 kg. | 2,250 lb. 1,020 kg. | 2,070 lb. 939 kg. |
| Whale Shark | Basking Shark | Great White Shark | Greenland Shark | Tiger Shark |

Whale sharks grow to an average of 30 feet (9 m) in length, but many have been known to reach up to 60 feet (18 m) long. That's the same length as two school buses! Whale sharks also weigh an average of 50,000 pounds (22, 680 kg). Amazingly, these gigantic fish eat only microscopic plankton and tiny fish. Whale sharks are usually found in tropical waters, where they float near the surface looking for food. Because they have very small teeth and are slow swimmers, these sharks are not a threat to humans.

# World's
# Fastest Fish

**THE WORLD'S FASTEST FISH**

Recorded speed in miles/kilometers per hour

| Fish | Speed |
|------|-------|
| Sailfish | 68 mph / 109 kph |
| Marlin | 50 mph / 80 kph |
| Bluefin Tuna | 46 mph / 74 kph |
| Yellowfin Tuna | 44 mph / 70 kph |
| Blue Shark | 43 mph / 69 kph |

# Sailfish

Although it is difficult to measure the exact speed of fish, a sailfish once grabbed a fishing line and dragged it 300 feet (91 m) away in just 3 seconds. That means it was swimming at an average speed of 68 miles (109 km) per hour—just higher than the average speed limit on the highway! Sailfish are very large—they average 6 feet (1.8 m) long, but can grow up to 11 feet (3.4 m). Like their swordfish relatives, they also have a long spear at the end of their snouts. The sailfish got its name from the long, blue dorsal fins on its back.

# World's Slowest Fish

## Sea Horse

Sea horses move around the ocean at just .001 miles (.002 km) per hour. At that rate of speed, it would take the fish about an hour to swim only 50 feet (15 m). Sea horses spend most of their time near the shore. There, they can hold on to plants with their tails. This helps them avoid enemies and prevents them from getting swept away by the tides. Sea horses are able to hover in the water by beating their dorsal fins about 35 times per second. This fin helps propel the fish forward.

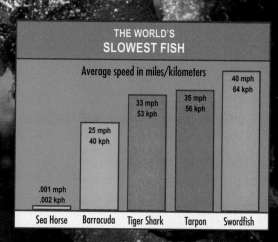

THE WORLD'S
SLOWEST FISH

Average speed in miles/kilometers

| Sea Horse | Barracuda | Tiger Shark | Tarpon | Swordfish |
|---|---|---|---|---|
| .001 mph .002 kph | 25 mph 40 kph | 33 mph 53 kph | 35 mph 56 kph | 40 mph 64 kph |

# World's Longest-Lived
# Ocean Creature

## Quahog

A quahog is a kind of marine clam that can live for about 200 years. That means some of the quahogs sitting on the ocean bottom today began their lives before the Civil War. Northern quahogs—also known as cherrystone clams, little-neck clams, and hard-shell clams—measure, on average, from 3 to 5 inches (8 to 12 cm) long. They are found in a region that stretches from the Gulf of St. Lawrence to the Gulf of Mexico. Southern quahogs are found from the Chesapeake Bay to the West Indies and grow 3 to 6 inches (7 to 15 cm) long. Both species have thick, white shells.

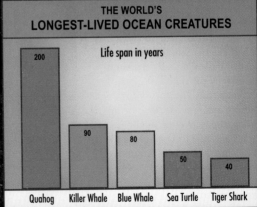

**THE WORLD'S LONGEST-LIVED OCEAN CREATURES**

Life span in years

| Quahog | Killer Whale | Blue Whale | Sea Turtle | Tiger Shark |
|--------|--------------|------------|------------|-------------|
| 200 | 90 | 80 | 50 | 40 |

# World's Largest Spider

## Goliath Birdeater

**THE WORLD'S LARGEST SPIDERS**

Length in inches/centimeters

| Goliath Birdeater | Salmon Pink Birdeater | Slate Red Ornamental | King Baboon | Colombian Giant Redleg |
|---|---|---|---|---|
| 11 in. 28 cm. | 10.5 in. 27 cm. | 9 in. 23 cm. | 8 in. 20 cm. | 8 in. 20 cm. |

A Goliath birdeater can grow to a total length of 11 inches (28 cm) and weigh about 6 ounces (170 g). A Goliath's spiderlings are also big—they can have a 6-inch (15-cm) leg span in just 1 year. These giant tarantulas are found mostly in the rain forests of Guyana, Suriname, Brazil, and Venezuela. The Goliath birdeater's name is misleading—they commonly eat insects and small reptiles. They are very aggressive spiders, and are able to stick enemies with their prickly hairs when alarmed, which is painful to humans but not harmful.

# World's
# Fastest Flying Insect

## Hawk Moth

The hawk moth got its name from its swift and steady flight. The average hawk moth can cruise along at speeds of up to 33 miles (53 km) per hour. That's faster than the average speed limit on most city streets. Also known as the sphinx moth and the hummingbird moth, this large insect can have a wingspan that reaches up to 8 inches (20 cm). Although they are found throughout the world, most species live in tropical climates. When alarmed, one species can produce loud squawking noises by blowing air through its tongue.

### THE WORLD'S
### FASTEST FLYING INSECTS

Speed in miles/kilometers per hour

| Hawk Moth | West Indian Butterfly | Deer Bot Fly | Dragonfly | Hornet |
|-----------|----------------------|--------------|-----------|--------|
| 33.3 mph 53.6 kph | 30.0 mph 48.2 kph | 30.0 mph 48.2 kph | 17.8 mph 28.6 kph | 13.3 mph 21.4 kph |

# World's Largest Moth

The atlas moth of New Guinea and Australia has a wingspan of almost 12 inches (31 cm). That's about the size of a dinner plate. In fact, atlas moths are often mistaken for birds when they are in flight. Their larvae are also gigantic—most measure about 11 inches (28 cm) long. The silk from an atlas moth cocoon is strong and is used to make certain kinds of clothing. Female atlas moths are slightly larger than males and rarely live longer than a month. Because they have no mouth parts to eat with, the only nutrition they get is from the fat deposits in their body.

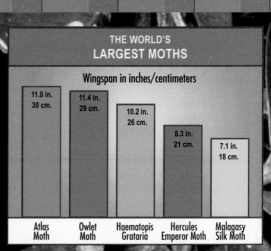

THE WORLD'S LARGEST MOTHS

Wingspan in inches/centimeters

| Atlas Moth | Owlet Moth | Haematopis Grataria | Hercules Emperor Moth | Malagasy Silk Moth |
|---|---|---|---|---|
| 11.8 in. 30 cm. | 11.4 in. 29 cm. | 10.2 in. 26 cm. | 8.3 in. 21 cm. | 7.1 in. 18 cm. |

## Atlas Moth

# World's Longest Insect

## Stick Insect

This tropical insect can grow to more than 22 inches (56 cm) in length. That is almost the same size as an average television screen. All together, there are about 2,000 species of stick insects. Most have long, thin brown or green bodies. Their twiglike appearance camouflages them well. When they are still, stick insects look just like part of a plant or tree. Some have colorful wings or sharp spines. Others are capable of spraying a foul odor when they are frightened or angry. All stick insects have the ability to grow back a leg or antenna that has broken off.

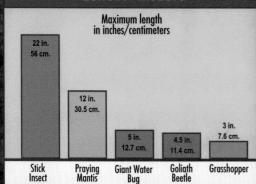

**THE WORLD'S LONGEST INSECTS**

Maximum length
in inches/centimeters

| Stick Insect | Praying Mantis | Giant Water Bug | Goliath Beetle | Grasshopper |
|---|---|---|---|---|
| 22 in. 56 cm. | 12 in. 30.5 cm. | 5 in. 12.7 cm. | 4.5 in. 11.4 cm. | 3 in. 7.6 cm. |

# World's Sleepiest Animal

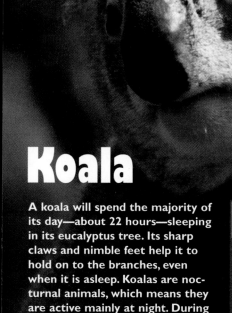

## Koala

A koala will spend the majority of its day—about 22 hours—sleeping in its eucalyptus tree. Its sharp claws and nimble feet help it to hold on to the branches, even when it is asleep. Koalas are nocturnal animals, which means they are active mainly at night. During the 2 hours a koala is awake, it will feed on 1 to 2 pounds (.4 to .9 kg) of eucalyptus leaves. A koala never needs to drink water; it gets enough liquid from its food. An average koala is about 2 feet (.6 m) tall and weighs about 22 pounds (10 kg).

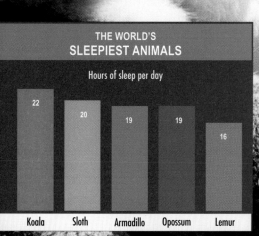

### THE WORLD'S SLEEPIEST ANIMALS

Hours of sleep per day

| Koala | Sloth | Armadillo | Opossum | Lemur |
|-------|-------|-----------|---------|-------|
| 22 | 20 | 19 | 19 | 16 |

# World's
# Fastest Land Mammal

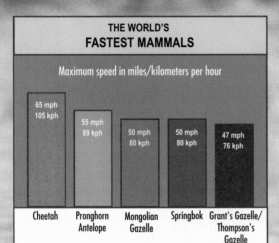

**THE WORLD'S FASTEST MAMMALS**

Maximum speed in miles/kilometers per hour

| | | | | |
|---|---|---|---|---|
| 65 mph 105 kph | 55 mph 89 kph | 50 mph 80 kph | 50 mph 80 kph | 47 mph 76 kph |
| Cheetah | Pronghorn Antelope | Mongolian Gazelle | Springbok | Grant's Gazelle/ Thompson's Gazelle |

These sleek mammals can reach a speed of 65 miles (105 km) per hour for short spurts. Their quickness enables these large African cats to easily outrun their prey. Some humans have even trained cheetahs to catch animals for them. Cheetahs are fairly easy to tame, even when captured as adults. Unlike the paws of all other cats, cheetah paws do not have skin sheaths—thin protective coverings. Their claws, therefore, cannot pull back.

## Cheetah

# World's
# Slowest Land Mammal

## Sloth

When a three-toed sloth is traveling on the ground, it reaches a top speed of only .07 miles (.11 km) per hour. That means that it would take the animal almost 15 minutes to cross a four-lane street. The main reason sloths move so slowly is that they cannot walk like other mammals. They must pull themselves along the ground using only their sharp claws. For this reason, sloths spend the majority of their time in trees. There, these animals are well camouflaged and can move from limb to limb as they feed on leaves.

### THE WORLD'S SLOWEST ANIMALS

Maximum speed in miles/kilometers per hour

|  |  |
| --- | --- |
| Sloth | .07 mph / .11 kph |
| Spider | 1.2 mph / 1.9 kph |
| Chicken | 9 mph / 14 kph |
| Pig | 11 mph / 18 kph |
| Squirrel | 12 mph / 19 kph |

# World's
# Smallest Mammal

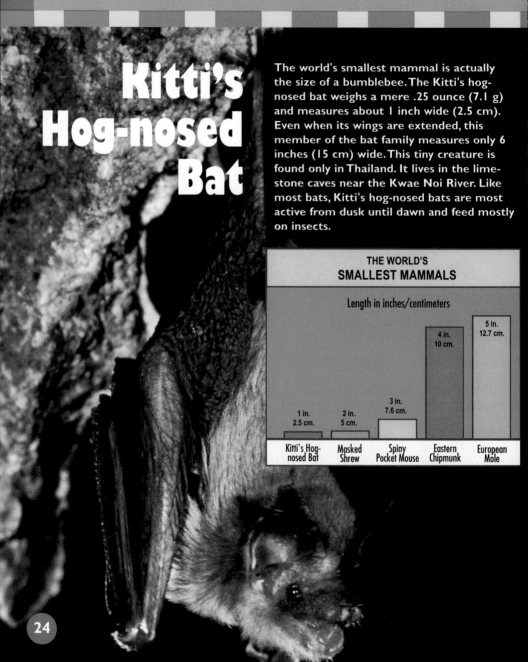

# Kitti's Hog-nosed Bat

The world's smallest mammal is actually the size of a bumblebee. The Kitti's hog-nosed bat weighs a mere .25 ounce (7.1 g) and measures about 1 inch wide (2.5 cm). Even when its wings are extended, this member of the bat family measures only 6 inches (15 cm) wide. This tiny creature is found only in Thailand. It lives in the limestone caves near the Kwae Noi River. Like most bats, Kitti's hog-nosed bats are most active from dusk until dawn and feed mostly on insects.

## THE WORLD'S SMALLEST MAMMALS

Length in inches/centimeters

| Kitti's Hog-nosed Bat | Masked Shrew | Spiny Pocket Mouse | Eastern Chipmunk | European Mole |
|---|---|---|---|---|
| 1 in. 2.5 cm. | 2 in. 5 cm. | 3 in. 7.6 cm. | 4 in. 10 cm. | 5 in. 12.7 cm. |

# World's Tallest Land Mammal

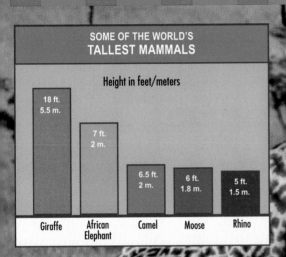

**SOME OF THE WORLD'S TALLEST MAMMALS**

Height in feet/meters

| Giraffe | African Elephant | Camel | Moose | Rhino |
|---|---|---|---|---|
| 18 ft. 5.5 m. | 7 ft. 2 m. | 6.5 ft. 2 m. | 6 ft. 1.8 m. | 5 ft. 1.5 m. |

# Giraffe

Giraffes can grow to more than 18 feet (5.5 m) in height. That means an average giraffe could look through the window of a two-story building. A giraffe's neck is 18 times longer than a human's, but both mammals have exactly the same number of neck bones. A giraffe's height and neck length allow it to feed on tall trees that other animals cannot reach. When it finds a tasty bud or leaf to eat, a giraffe will use its 18-inch (46-cm) tongue to grab it.

# World's Heaviest
# Marine Mammal

## Blue Whale

These enormous sea creatures can measure more than 100 feet (30 m) long and weigh more than 143 tons (129.7 t), making them the largest animals that have ever lived. Amazingly, these gentle giants only eat krill—small, shrimplike animals. During the summer, when food is plentiful, a blue whale can eat about 4 tons (3.6 t) of krill each day. To catch the krill, a whale gulps as much as 17,000 gallons (64,600 l) of seawater into its mouth at one time. Then it uses its tongue—which can be the same size as a car— to push the water back out. The krill get caught in hairs on the whale's baleen (a keratin structure that hangs down from the roof of the whale's mouth).

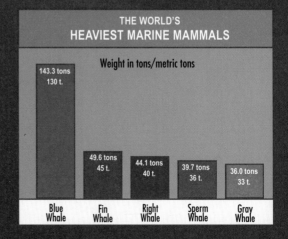

**THE WORLD'S HEAVIEST MARINE MAMMALS**

Weight in tons/metric tons

- Blue Whale: 143.3 tons / 130 t.
- Fin Whale: 49.6 tons / 45 t.
- Right Whale: 44.1 tons / 40 t.
- Sperm Whale: 39.7 tons / 36 t.
- Gray Whale: 36.0 tons / 33 t.

# World's Heaviest Land Mammal

## African Elephant

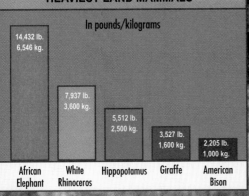

**THE WORLD'S HEAVIEST LAND MAMMALS**

In pounds/kilograms

|  |  |
| --- | --- |
| African Elephant | 14,432 lb. / 6,546 kg. |
| White Rhinoceros | 7,937 lb. / 3,600 kg. |
| Hippopotamus | 5,512 lb. / 2,500 kg. |
| Giraffe | 3,527 lb. / 1,600 kg. |
| American Bison | 2,205 lb. / 1,000 kg. |

African elephants measure approximately 24 feet (7.3 m) long and can weigh up to 6 tons (5.4 t). Even at their great size, they are strictly vegetarian—they eat only twigs, foliage, fruit, and grasses. They will, however, eat up to 500 pounds (226 kg) of vegetation a day! Elephants have only four teeth with which to chew their food, but each tooth is a whopping 12 inches (31 cm) in length! Their two tusks—which are really elongated teeth—grow continuously during their lives and can reach about 9 feet (2.7 m) in length.

# World's
# Largest Rodent

## Capybara

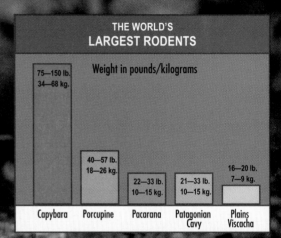

**THE WORLD'S
LARGEST RODENTS**

Weight in pounds/kilograms

| | | | | |
|---|---|---|---|---|
| 75—150 lb. 34—68 kg. | 40—57 lb. 18—26 kg. | 22—33 lb. 10—15 kg. | 21—33 lb. 10—15 kg. | 16—20 lb. 7—9 kg. |
| Capybara | Porcupine | Pacarana | Patagonian Cavy | Plains Viscacha |

Also known as water hogs and carpinchos, capybaras reach an average length of 4 feet (1.2 m), stand about 20 inches (51 cm) tall, and weigh between 75 and 150 pounds (34 to 68 kg)! That's about the same size as a Labrador retriever. Capybaras are found in South and Central America, where they spend much of their time in groups looking for food. They are strictly vegetarian, and have been known to raid gardens for melons and squash. Their partially webbed feet make capybaras excellent swimmers.

# World's Longest-Lived
# Mammal

# Killer Whale

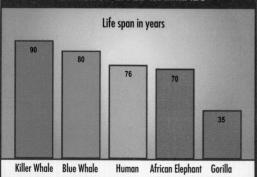

## THE WORLD'S LONGEST-LIVED MAMMALS

### Life span in years

| Killer Whale | Blue Whale | Human | African Elephant | Gorilla |
|---|---|---|---|---|
| 90 | 80 | 76 | 70 | 35 |

The average life span of a killer whale is 90 years. The average life span of a human is only about 76 years. Killer whales, also known as orcas, hold the record as the world's largest meat eater as well. Males can measure up to 28 feet (9m) long and weigh up to 12,000 pounds (5,443 kg). Some of these whales have been known to eat up to 2,000 pounds (907 kg) in just one feeding. These giant creatures can be found in every ocean.

# World's
# Deadliest Snake

## Black Mamba

Just one bite from an African black mamba snake releases a venom powerful enough to kill up to 200 humans. If it is not treated immediately, a bite from this snake is almost always fatal. This large member of the cobra family grows to about 14 feet (4.3 m) long. Depending on its age, it can range in color from gray to green to black. In addition to its deadly poison, it is also a very aggressive snake. It will raise its body off the ground when it feels threatened. It then spreads its hood and strikes swiftly at its prey with its long front teeth.

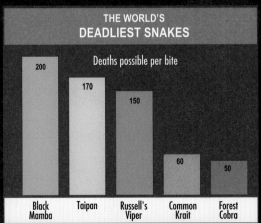

THE WORLD'S
DEADLIEST SNAKES

Deaths possible per bite

| Black Mamba | Taipan | Russell's Viper | Common Krait | Forest Cobra |
|---|---|---|---|---|
| 200 | 170 | 150 | 60 | 50 |

# World's Most
# Deadly Amphibian

## Poison Dart Frog

Even though they measure only .5 to 2 inches (1 to 5 cm) long, these lethal amphibians have enough poison in their skin to kill up to 20 adult humans. A dart frog's poison is so effective that native Central and South Americans sometimes coat their hunting arrows or hunting darts with it. Poison dart frogs are found mostly in the tropical rain forests of Central and South America, where they live on the moist land. These brightly colored frogs can be yellow, orange, red, green, blue, or any combination of these colors. They feed mostly on beetles, ants, termites, and other insects by capturing them with their sticky tongues.

### SOME OF THE WORLD'S
### POISONOUS AMPHIBIANS

Length in inches/centimeters

| | | | | |
|---|---|---|---|---|
| 2 in. 5.1 cm. | 2.5 in. 6.4 cm. | 3 in. 7.6 cm. | 4 in. 10 cm. | 10 in. 25.4 cm. |
| Poison Dart Frog | Black and Yellow Spotted Frog | Fire-bellied Toad | European Salamander | Canetoad |

# World's
# Longest Snake

## Reticulated Python

The average adult reticulated python is about 17 feet (5 m) long, but some can grow to more than 27 feet (8.2 m) in length. That's almost the length of an average school bus. These pythons live mostly in Asia, from Myanmar to Indonesia to the Philippines. They spend much of their time near riverbanks, but some can be found in cities. Reticulated pythons are slow-moving creatures that kill their prey by constriction, or strangulation. They are capable of swallowing animals as large as goats and pigs, but usually stalk much smaller animals.

THE WORLD'S
**LONGEST SNAKES**

Length in feet/meters

| Reticulated Python | Anaconda | Rock Python | King Cobra | Oriental Rat Snake |
|---|---|---|---|---|
| 27 ft. 8.2 m. | 25 ft. 7.6 m. | 24.6 ft. 7.5 m. | 17.7 ft. 5.4 m. | 12.2 ft. 3.7 m. |

# World's Largest Lizard

## Komodo Dragon

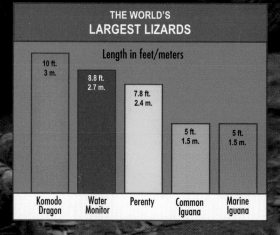

### THE WORLD'S LARGEST LIZARDS

**Length in feet/meters**

| Komodo Dragon | Water Monitor | Perenty | Common Iguana | Marine Iguana |
|---|---|---|---|---|
| 10 ft. 3 m. | 8.8 ft. 2.7 m. | 7.8 ft. 2.4 m. | 5 ft. 1.5 m. | 5 ft. 1.5 m. |

These large members of the monitor family can grow to 10 feet (3 m) in length and weigh about 300 pounds (136 kg). A Komodo dragon has a long neck and tail, and strong legs. They are found mainly on Komodo Island, but some can still be found on other islands in Indonesia. Komodos are dangerous and have even been known to attack and kill humans. When it is feeding, a Komodo can eat a meal equal to one-half its body weight in less than 20 minutes. In fact, a Komodo can consume 80% of its body weight in just one meal!

# World's
# Largest Reptile

## Saltwater Crocodile

These enormous reptiles can measure more than 22 feet (6.7 m) long. That's about twice the length of the average car. However, males usually measure only about 17 feet (5 m) long, and females normally reach about 10 feet (3 m) in length. Saltwater crocodiles are found throughout the East Indies and Australia. They are strong swimmers and can spend a great deal of time at sea. Because they have been at sea so long, barnacles have even been found on the scales of some of these animals. Despite their name, saltwater crocodiles can also be found in freshwater and swamps.

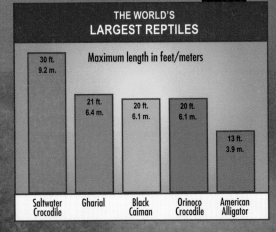

THE WORLD'S
LARGEST REPTILES

Maximum length in feet/meters

| Saltwater Crocodile | Gharial | Black Caiman | Orinoco Crocodile | American Alligator |
|---|---|---|---|---|
| 30 ft. 9.2 m. | 21 ft. 6.4 m. | 20 ft. 6.1 m. | 20 ft. 6.1 m. | 13 ft. 3.9 m. |

# World's Largest Turtle

## Pacific Leatherback

### THE WORLD'S LARGEST TURTLES

Weight in pounds/kilograms

| | | | | |
|---|---|---|---|---|
| 1,900 lb. 862 kg. | 1,000 lb. 454 kg. | 900 lb. 408 kg. | 850 lb. 386 kg. | 403 lb. 183 kg. |
| Pacific Leatherback | Atlantic Leatherback | Green Sea Turtle | Loggerhead Turtle | Alligator Snapping Turtle |

These giant sea turtles can grow up to 7 feet (2.1 m) long and weigh up to 1,900 pounds (862 kg). They also measure about 9 feet (2.7 m) from the tip of one flipper to the tip of the other. These powerful flippers allow the turtle to move swiftly through the water. Although Pacific leatherbacks spend the majority of their time in the water, they migrate over very long distances to lay their eggs on certain beaches. These turtles do have shells, even though they are not clearly visible. The shell consists of bones and is buried under the turtle's thick skin.

# World's Longest-Lived Reptile

## Galápagos Turtle

Some of these giant reptiles have been known to live for more than 150 years. Amazingly, Galápagos turtles can go without eating or drinking for many weeks. This is partly because it can take them up to three weeks to digest a meal! Galápagos turtles are also some of the largest turtles in the world, weighing in at up to 500 pounds (226 kg). Sadly, these gentle animals are in danger of extinction. Worldwide, there are fewer than 15,000 members of the species alive today.

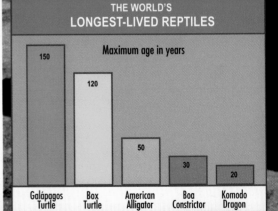

THE WORLD'S
LONGEST-LIVED REPTILES

Maximum age in years

| Galápagos Turtle | Box Turtle | American Alligator | Boa Constrictor | Komodo Dragon |
|---|---|---|---|---|
| 150 | 120 | 50 | 30 | 20 |

# Deadliest Twentieth-Century
# Floods

## Huang He River

### THE TWENTIETH CENTURY'S DEADLIEST FLOODS

**Estimated deaths**

| Huang He River, China 1931 | Bangladesh, 1970 | Henan, China 1939 | Chang Jiang River, China 1911 | Bengal, India 1942 |
|---|---|---|---|---|
| 3.7 M | 500,000 | 200,000 | 100,000 | 40,000 |

The powerful floodwaters from the Huang He, or Yellow River, in China burst through villages and towns in August of 1931, killing an estimated 3.7 million people. It was not the first time the Huang He has caused disaster. This 3,000-mile-(4,828-km) long river has flooded its surrounding areas more than 1,500 times in the last 1,800 years. It has even changed its course nine times. The Chinese have tried building dams, dikes, and overflow channels to control the river, but during the summer flood season, many of the structures collapse under the immense pressure of the surging waters.

# Deadliest Twentieth-Century
# Hurricane

## Hurricane Mitch

Beginning on October 26, 1998, Hurricane Mitch pounded Central America, killing more than 11,000 people and causing more than $3 billion in damage. The countries hit hardest were Nicaragua and Honduras, but El Salvador and Guatemala also sustained significant damage. Besides the gusting winds and pouring rain, giant mudslides and raging floods destroyed millions of homes and took thousands of lives. Many of those who survived this terrible storm were faced with the resulting cholera epidemic.

### THE TWENTIETH CENTURY'S
### DEADLIEST HURRICANES

**Estimated deaths**

| Hurricane Mitch, 1998 | Galveston, Texas, 1900 | Hurricane Fifi, 1974 | Dominican Republic, 1930 | Hurricane Flora, 1963 |
|---|---|---|---|---|
| 11,000 | 8,000 | 8,000 | 8,000 | 7,200 |

# Deadliest Twentieth-Century Cyclone

# East Pakistan, 1970

After the cyclone swept through Bangladesh, formerly East Pakistan, on November 12, 1970, more than 200,000 people were dead and 100,000 people were missing. Violent winds destroyed houses and crops, and caused devastating tidal waves. Because the country is small and very densely populated, storms such as these often create a high death toll. East Pakistan was one of the world's poorest countries, which meant that rebuilding after this storm was a slow process that ultimately took decades and required help from countries around the world.

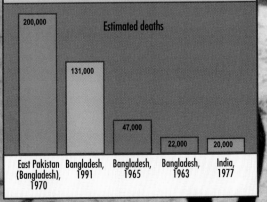

**THE TWENTIETH CENTURY'S DEADLIEST CYCLONES**

Estimated deaths

| | Estimated deaths |
|---|---|
| East Pakistan (Bangladesh), 1970 | 200,000 |
| Bangladesh, 1991 | 131,000 |
| Bangladesh, 1965 | 47,000 |
| Bangladesh, 1963 | 22,000 |
| India, 1977 | 20,000 |

# Deadliest Twentieth-Century Earthquake

# Tangshan

On July 28, 1976, Tangshan, China, was rocked by an earthquake that killed more than 242,000 people. The tragedy devastated the city, killing or seriously injuring one-quarter of its total population. Since that time, Tangshan has come to be known as the "Brave City of China" because of its successful rebuilding efforts. With its new earthquake-proof buildings and an impressive high-tech transportation system, the city now plays an important role in China's economy. Tangshan is a major supplier of fish, iron ore, and produce.

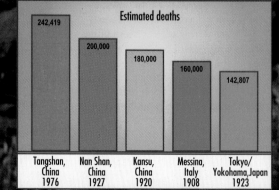

## THE TWENTIETH CENTURY'S DEADLIEST EARTHQUAKES

### Estimated deaths

| Tangshan, China 1976 | Nan Shan, China 1927 | Kansu, China 1920 | Messina, Italy 1908 | Tokyo/ Yokohama, Japan 1923 |
|---|---|---|---|---|
| 242,419 | 200,000 | 180,000 | 160,000 | 142,807 |

# Mount Pelée

Mount Pelée is located on the small island of Martinique in the Caribbean Sea. When this volcano erupted on May 8, 1902, it killed about 30,000 people, mostly with its tremendously hot ash flows. By the time the eruption subsided, about 15% of the island's population had been killed. The flows also destroyed the port and town of Saint-Pierre, the island's business center. After the eruption, much of the town was not rebuilt, and many ruins are still visible. The 4,583-foot- (1,397-m) tall volcanic mountain most recently erupted in 1929, but caused little damage.

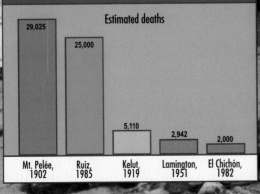

**THE TWENTIETH CENTURY'S DEADLIEST VOLCANIC ERUPTIONS**

Estimated deaths

| Eruption | Estimated deaths |
|---|---|
| Mt. Pelée, 1902 | 29,025 |
| Ruiz, 1985 | 25,000 |
| Kelut, 1919 | 5,110 |
| Lamington, 1951 | 2,942 |
| El Chichón, 1982 | 2,000 |

# World's Top Calorie-Consuming Country

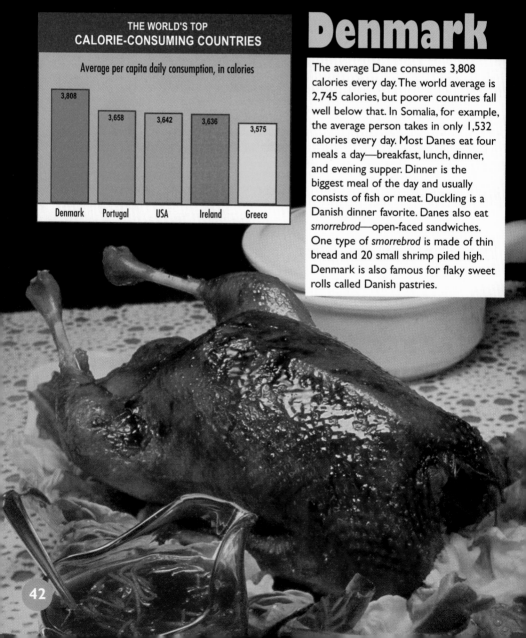

## THE WORLD'S TOP CALORIE-CONSUMING COUNTRIES

Average per capita daily consumption, in calories

| Denmark | Portugal | USA | Ireland | Greece |
|---------|----------|-----|---------|--------|
| 3,808 | 3,658 | 3,642 | 3,636 | 3,575 |

# Denmark

The average Dane consumes 3,808 calories every day. The world average is 2,745 calories, but poorer countries fall well below that. In Somalia, for example, the average person takes in only 1,532 calories every day. Most Danes eat four meals a day—breakfast, lunch, dinner, and evening supper. Dinner is the biggest meal of the day and usually consists of fish or meat. Duckling is a Danish dinner favorite. Danes also eat *smorrebrod*—open-faced sandwiches. One type of *smorrebrod* is made of thin bread and 20 small shrimp piled high. Denmark is also famous for flaky sweet rolls called Danish pastries.

# World's
# Largest Fruit

## Pumpkin

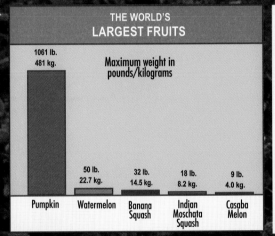

**THE WORLD'S LARGEST FRUITS**

Maximum weight in pounds/kilograms

| Pumpkin | Watermelon | Banana Squash | Indian Moschata Squash | Casaba Melon |
|---|---|---|---|---|
| 1061 lb. 481 kg. | 50 lb. 22.7 kg. | 32 lb. 14.5 kg. | 18 lb. 8.2 kg. | 9 lb. 4.0 kg. |

Although the average size of a pumpkin can vary greatly depending on the variety and species, the greatest weight ever attained by a fruit belongs to a pumpkin. The largest pumpkin ever grown (and recorded) weighed a remarkable 1,061 pounds (481 kg). Pumpkins are grown throughout North America, Great Britain, and Europe for both human consumption and livestock feed. In the United States, pumpkins are used mainly in pies, soups, and puddings. In Europe, pumpkin is usually served as a meal's side dish.

# World's Largest Vegetable

## Yam

Some specially grown vegetables have been recorded at higher weights than the largest yam, but true yams can consistently grow up to 9 feet (2.7 m) long and weigh more than 150 pounds (68 kg). No other vegetable can consistently reach this size and weight. Even though these giant tropical tuber roots are capable of reaching such a great size, they are usually harvested when they reach about 6 pounds (2.7 kg). While yams are a major food crop in several countries, some varieties are more valuable for the medicinal ingredient they produce.

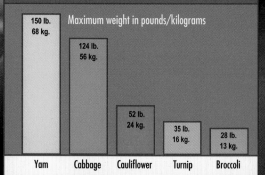

THE WORLD'S
LARGEST VEGETABLES

Maximum weight in pounds/kilograms

| | | | | |
|---|---|---|---|---|
| 150 lb. 68 kg. | 124 lb. 56 kg. | 52 lb. 24 kg. | 35 lb. 16 kg. | 28 lb. 13 kg. |
| Yam | Cabbage | Cauliflower | Turnip | Broccoli |

# World's
# Smallest Vegetable

## Snow Pea

Snow peas measure only about .25 inch (.64 cm) in diameter. That's probably smaller than the size of your pinky fingernail. Snow pea pods are fairly flat and bright green in color. They grow to about 3 inches (7.5 cm) in length and hold 5 to 7 peas. Because of the pod's sweet flavor, it is usually eaten with the peas. Snow peas are eaten throughout the world, but they are especially popular in Asia and the United States. They are a good source of vitamins A and C, potassium, and iron.

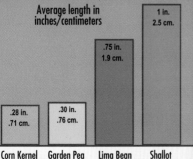

THE WORLD'S
SMALLEST VEGETABLES

Average length in inches/centimeters

| Snow Pea | Corn Kernel | Garden Pea | Lima Bean | Shallot |
|----------|-------------|------------|-----------|---------|
| .25 in. .64 cm. | .28 in. .71 cm. | .30 in. .76 cm. | .75 in. 1.9 cm. | 1 in. 2.5 cm. |

# World's Most Expensive Food

## Saffron

### THE WORLD'S MOST EXPENSIVE FOODS

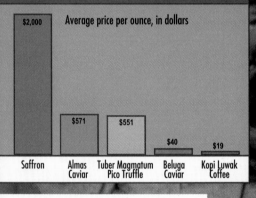

Average price per ounce, in dollars

| Saffron | Almas Caviar | Tuber Magmatum Pico Truffle | Beluga Caviar | Kopi Luwak Coffee |
|---------|--------------|-----------------------------|---------------|-------------------|
| $2,000 | $571 | $551 | $40 | $19 |

Just 1 ounce (28 g) of saffron is worth about $2,000. Because of its high value, this yellow spice is commonly sold in very small amounts, averaging about $4 for .002 ounce (.057 g). Saffron's high price tag is attributed to the painstaking process of obtaining it. Saffron comes from the inside of purple crocuses, which are small bulb plants that flower in the spring. Harvesting it takes a long time and is a very delicate procedure. To make just 1 pound (.45 kg) of saffron, about 70,000 to 250,000 flower stigmas must be collected by hand.

# Country That Eats the Most Chocolate

## Switzerland

In Switzerland, the average person consumes about 19 pounds (8.6 kg) of chocolate each year. That means approximately 138 million pounds (62 million kg) of chocolate is eaten in this small country annually. Chocolate is consumed mainly in the form of candy, but it is also used to make beverages, to flavor recipes, and to glaze various sweets and bakery products. Chocolate has always been a popular food around the world. In fact, each year, approximately 600,000 tons (544.320 t) of cocoa beans—an important ingredient in chocolate—are consumed worldwide.

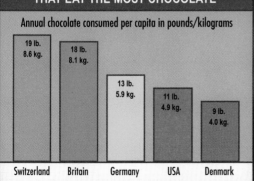

**THE WORLD'S COUNTRIES THAT EAT THE MOST CHOCOLATE**

Annual chocolate consumed per capita in pounds/kilograms

| | | | | |
|---|---|---|---|---|
| 19 lb. 8.6 kg. | 18 lb. 8.1 kg. | 13 lb. 5.9 kg. | 11 lb. 4.9 kg. | 9 lb. 4.0 kg. |
| Switzerland | Britain | Germany | USA | Denmark |

# Country That Drinks the Most Coffee

## Finland

During one year, the average person in Finland consumes more than 24 pounds (10.8 kg) of coffee. That's equal to 4.5 cups per day, or an amazing 1,650 cups a year. This means that approximately 8.5 billion cups—or 531.5 million gallons (2.01 billion l)—of coffee are sipped each year within the country. Coffee is also the most popular drink throughout the world. More than 400 billion cups are consumed each year. Coffee drinkers enjoy about one-half of all coffee with breakfast, and one-third is drunk between meals. Men drink slightly more coffee than women.

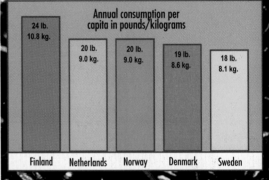

**THE WORLD'S COUNTRIES THAT DRINK THE MOST COFFEE**

Annual consumption per capita in pounds/kilograms

| Finland | Netherlands | Norway | Denmark | Sweden |
|---|---|---|---|---|
| 24 lb. 10.8 kg. | 20 lb. 9.0 kg. | 20 lb. 9.0 kg. | 19 lb. 8.6 kg. | 18 lb. 8.1 kg. |

# Country That Drinks the Most Milk

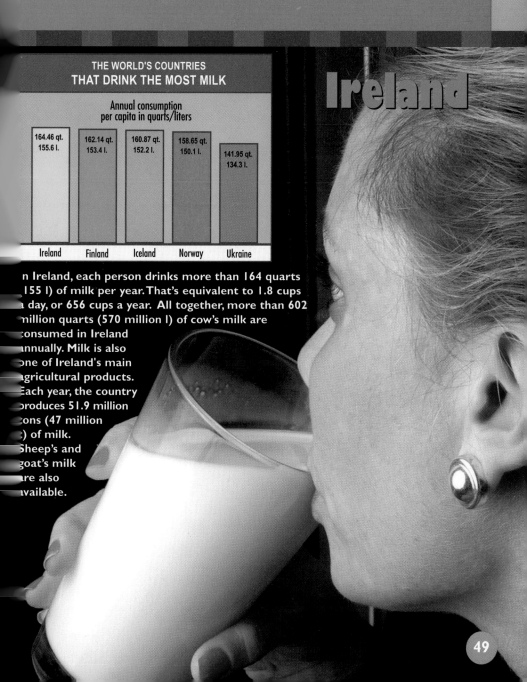

**THE WORLD'S COUNTRIES THAT DRINK THE MOST MILK**

Annual consumption per capita in quarts/liters

| Ireland | Finland | Iceland | Norway | Ukraine |
|---------|---------|---------|--------|---------|
| 164.46 qt. 155.6 l. | 162.14 qt. 153.4 l. | 160.87 qt. 152.2 l. | 158.65 qt. 150.1 l. | 141.95 qt. 134.3 l. |

**Ireland**

In Ireland, each person drinks more than 164 quarts (155 l) of milk per year. That's equivalent to 1.8 cups a day, or 656 cups a year. All together, more than 602 million quarts (570 million l) of cow's milk are consumed in Ireland annually. Milk is also one of Ireland's main agricultural products. Each year, the country produces 51.9 million tons (47 million t) of milk. Sheep's and goat's milk are also available.

49

# Country That Consumes the Most Sugar

## Israel

In Israel, about 216 pounds (98 kg) of sugar is consumed by each resident in just one year. That's the average weight of a 6-foot- (1.8-m) tall person. Sugar also can be found in many different types of foods. Junk foods like candy, cookies, and fast foods are loaded with sugar. Healthier foods, however, like vegetables and fruit juices, also contain high levels of natural sugars. Americans, by comparison, consume about 156 pounds (69 kg) of sugar per capita each year—much of which is from soft drinks.

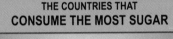

### THE COUNTRIES THAT CONSUME THE MOST SUGAR

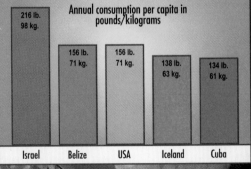

Annual consumption per capita in pounds/kilograms

| Israel | Belize | USA | Iceland | Cuba |
|--------|--------|-----|---------|------|
| 216 lb. 98 kg. | 156 lb. 71 kg. | 156 lb. 71 kg. | 138 lb. 63 kg. | 134 lb. 61 kg. |

# Country That Drinks the Most Coca-Cola

## Mexico

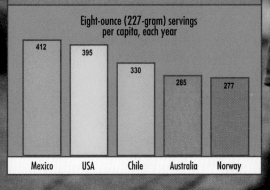

**THE COUNTRIES THAT DRINK THE MOST COCA-COLA PRODUCTS**

Eight-ounce (227-gram) servings per capita, each year

| Mexico | USA | Chile | Australia | Norway |
|--------|-----|-------|-----------|--------|
| 412 | 395 | 330 | 285 | 277 |

In an average year, each person living in Mexico consumes approximately 412 servings of Coca-Cola beverages. Coca-Cola, the global soft-drink industry leader, sells many brands that are well known throughout the world, including Coke and Sprite. But the company also sells special soft-drink brands to each area of the world. The popular flavors in Mexico include Fresca, a carbonated grapefruit drink; Delaware Punch, a non-carbonated grape drink; and Lift, a carbonated apple drink.

51

# World's Top
# Meat-Eating Country

# United States

In one year, each person in the United States will eat about 261 pounds (118.4 kg) of meat. That's the same weight as 75 phone books. The most commonly eaten meat in the U.S. is beef—about 64 pounds (29 kg) per person per year. In fact, an average 43 million pounds (19.5 million kg) of beef are eaten in the United States each day. A hamburger or cheeseburger is the most common way to eat beef—more than 85% of U.S. citizens ate at least one last year. Chicken is the second most popular, with each American eating about 50 pounds (22.6 kg) per year.

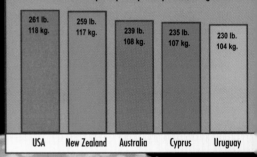

**THE COUNTRIES WITH THE HIGHEST MEAT CONSUMPTION**

Annual consumption per capita in pounds/kilograms

| USA | New Zealand | Australia | Cyprus | Uruguay |
|---|---|---|---|---|
| 261 lb. 118 kg. | 259 lb. 117 kg. | 239 lb. 108 kg. | 235 lb. 107 kg. | 230 lb. 104 kg. |

# World's Top
# Rice-Growing Country

## China

In just one year, China produces more than 212 million tons (192 t) of rice. This grain, in fact, is the most popular food crop grown throughout the world. It is usually grown in flooded fields called paddies. Transplanting the seedlings and harvesting the grain take a very long time. China produces many different kinds of rice. The higher quality rice is mainly consumed within the country. It is an important source of protein and calories in the Chinese diet. China also exports rice to other countries. The lower quality grain is fed to animals and livestock.

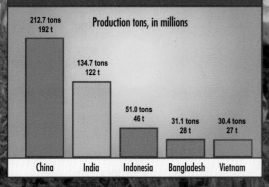

**COUNTRIES WITH THE HIGHEST RICE PRODUCTION**

Production tons, in millions

| Country | Production |
|---------|-----------|
| China | 212.7 tons / 192 t |
| India | 134.7 tons / 122 t |
| Indonesia | 51.0 tons / 46 t |
| Bangladesh | 31.1 tons / 28 t |
| Vietnam | 30.4 tons / 27 t |

# World's
# Largest Canyon

## Colca Canyon

### THE WORLD'S
### LARGEST CANYONS

**Depth in feet/meters**

| | | | | |
|---|---|---|---|---|
| 11,000 ft.<br>3,400 m. | | | | |
| | 9,842 ft.<br>3,000 m. | | | |
| | | 8,200 ft.<br>2,499 m. | | |
| | | | 5,280 ft.<br>1,609 m. | |
| | | | | 3,000 ft.<br>914 m. |
| Colca<br>Canyon,<br>Peru | Tiger Leaping<br>Gorge,<br>China | Kings<br>Canyon,<br>USA | Grand<br>Canyon,<br>USA | Rocky<br>Mountain Tren<br>USA/Canad |

Colca Canyon in Peru has a depth
11,000 feet (3,400 m). That's more
than twice the depth of the Grand
Canyon. Colca Canyon is 37.3 mile
(60 km) long. It extends from Chiva
Peru, in the east to Cabanaconde,
Peru, in the west. The canyon was
carved out by the Colca River
millions of years ago. About nine
villages line the edges of the canyo
and terraces, built by the Incas,
are found on the slopes. Andean
condors frequently fly around the
canyon and are a popular sight for
tourists.

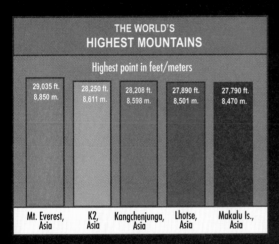

## THE WORLD'S HIGHEST MOUNTAINS

### Highest point in feet/meters

| Mt. Everest, Asia | K2, Asia | Kangchenjunga, Asia | Lhotse, Asia | Makalu Is., Asia |
|---|---|---|---|---|
| 29,035 ft. 8,850 m. | 28,250 ft. 8,611 m. | 28,208 ft. 8,598 m. | 27,890 ft. 8,501 m. | 27,790 ft. 8,470 m. |

Towering 29,035 feet (8,850 m) into the air, Mt. Everest's tallest peak is the highest point on Earth. This peak is an unbelievable 5.5 miles (8.8 km) above sea level. Mt. Everest is located in the Himalayas, on the border between Nepal and Tibet. In 1953, Sir Edmund Hillary and Tenzin Norgay were the first people to reach the peak. Since then, about 900 people have made it to the top.

# Mount Everest

# World's Deepest Lake

## Lake Baikal

This Russian lake is located in Siberia and has a maximum depth of 5,315 feet (1,620 m). That's deep enough to completely cover four Empire State buildings stacked one on top of the other. This lake is also the oldest fresh-water lake in the world, dating back almost 25 million years. By volume, Baikal is the world's largest freshwater lake. It is 395 miles (635 km) long, about 30 miles (48 km) wide, and covers an area of about 12,200 square miles (31,598 sq km). With its great size and volume, Lake Baikal holds about one-fifth of all the freshwater on Earth's surface.

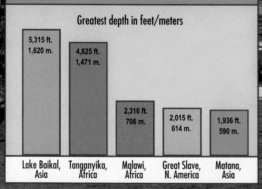

**THE WORLD'S DEEPEST LAKES**

Greatest depth in feet/meters

| Lake | Depth |
|------|-------|
| Lake Baikal, Asia | 5,315 ft. 1,620 m. |
| Tanganyika, Africa | 4,825 ft. 1,471 m. |
| Malawi, Africa | 2,316 ft. 706 m. |
| Great Slave, N. America | 2,015 ft. 614 m. |
| Matana, Asia | 1,936 ft. 590 m. |

# World's
# Largest Ocean

## Pacific

The Pacific Ocean covers almost 64 million square miles (166 million sq km), and reaches 36,200 feet (11,000 m) below sea level at its greatest depth—the Mariana Trench (near the Philippines). In fact, this ocean is so large that it covers about one-third of the planet (more than all of Earth's land put together) and holds more than half of all the seawater on Earth, about 6 sextillion (21 zeros) gallons (23 sextillion l). The Pacific also has the world's largest ocean current, the Kuroshio Current. The Kuroshio can travel up to 75 miles (120 km) a day and reach a depth of 3,300 feet (1,005 m).

### THE WORLD'S LARGEST OCEANS

Maximum area in millions of square miles/square kilometers

| Pacific Ocean | Atlantic Ocean | Indian Ocean | Arctic Ocean |
|---|---|---|---|
| 64 M sq. mi. 165.7 M sq. km. | 31.8 M sq. mi. 82.4 M sq. km. | 25.3 M sq. mi. 65.5 M sq. km. | 5.4 M sq. mi. 14.0 M sq. km. |

# World's
# Largest Desert

## The Sahara

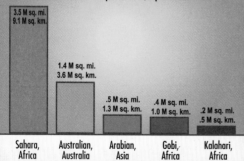

### THE WORLD'S LARGEST DESERTS

Area in millions of square miles/square kilometers

| Desert | Area |
|---|---|
| Sahara, Africa | 3.5 M sq. mi. / 9.1 M sq. km. |
| Australian, Australia | 1.4 M sq. mi. / 3.6 M sq. km. |
| Arabian, Asia | .5 M sq. mi. / 1.3 M sq. km. |
| Gobi, Africa | .4 M sq. mi. / 1.0 M sq. km. |
| Kalahari, Africa | .2 M sq. mi. / .5 M sq. km. |

The Sahara Desert in northern Africa covers approximately 3.5 million square miles (9.1 million sq km). It stretches for 5,200 miles (1,585 km) through the countries of Morocco, Algeria, Tunisia, Libya, Egypt, Mauritania, Mali, Niger, Chad, and Sudan. The Sahara gets very little rainfall—less than 8 inches (20 cm) per year. Although summer daytime temperatures can reach 136° Fahrenheit (58° C), the nights and winters are cold. In fact, some areas in the higher elevations even have snow-capped peaks in the winter!

# World's
# Largest Lake

# Caspian Sea

This giant inland body of saltwater stretches for almost 750 miles (1,207 km) from north to south, with an average width of about 200 miles (322 km). All together, it covers an area that's almost the same size as the state of California. The Caspian Sea is located east of the Caucasus Mountains in Central Asia. It is bordered by Iran, Russia, Kazakhstan, Azerbaijan, and Turkmenistan. It has a maximum depth of 3,360 feet (1,024 m) near its southern coast.

## THE WORLD'S
## LARGEST LAKES

Approximate area in square miles/square kilometers

| Caspian Sea, Asia | Superior, N. America | Victoria, Africa | Huron, N. America | Michigan, N. America |
|---|---|---|---|---|
| 143,205 sq. mi. 370,901 sq. km. | 31,820 sq. mi. 82,413 sq. km. | 26,570 sq. mi. 68,816 sq. km. | 23,010 sq. mi. 59,596 sq. km. | 22,400 sq. mi. 58,016 sq. km. |

# World's Tallest
# Active Volcano

## Guallatiri

The Guallatiri volcano towers an amazing 19,918 feet (6,071 m) into the sky. That means it is approximately 132 times taller than the Statue of Liberty. Guallatiri is located in northern Chile, near the border of Bolivia. Its last eruption, which caused relatively little disturbance, took place in 1987. Guallatiri is classified as a stratovolcano, which means it is made from exploded cinder, ash, and lava flows.

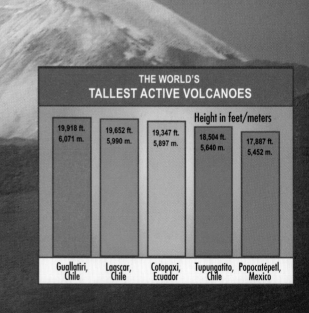

### THE WORLD'S TALLEST ACTIVE VOLCANOES

Height in feet/meters

| Guallatiri, Chile | Laascar, Chile | Cotopaxi, Ecuador | Tupungatito, Chile | Popocatépetl, Mexico |
|---|---|---|---|---|
| 19,918 ft. 6,071 m. | 19,652 ft. 5,990 m. | 19,347 ft. 5,897 m. | 18,504 ft. 5,640 m. | 17,887 ft. 5,452 m. |

# World's Deepest Land Depression

## Dead Sea

*Chinese President Jiang Zemin swimming in the Dead Sea*

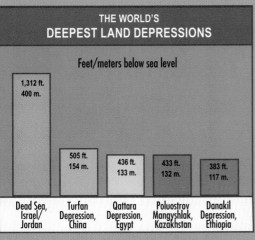

### THE WORLD'S DEEPEST LAND DEPRESSIONS

Feet/meters below sea level

| Dead Sea, Israel/ Jordan | Turfan Depression, China | Qattara Depression, Egypt | Poluostrov Mangyshlak, Kazakhstan | Danakil Depression, Ethiopia |
|---|---|---|---|---|
| 1,312 ft. 400 m. | 505 ft. 154 m. | 436 ft. 133 m. | 433 ft. 132 m. | 383 ft. 117 m. |

Located on the border of Israel and Jordan, the shore of this saltwater lake lies 1,312 feet (400 m) below sea level. The lake bottom reaches depths as great as 2,622 feet (799 m) below sea level. The Dead Sea is situated in the deepest underwater trench in the Great Rift Valley. Its coastline is about 46 miles (74 km) long and about 10 miles (16 km) wide. The water in this lake is about seven times saltier than ocean water, which is why almost nothing but the simplest organisms can live in it. The salt makes the water so dense that people can easily float in it. Approximately 55 inches (140 cm) of water evaporate from the lake every year, causing the water level to vary up to 2 feet .6 m) during the year.

# World's Highest Waterfall

## Angel Falls

This spectacular 3,212-foot- (979-m) high waterfall is located on the Churun River in the Guiana Highlands of southeastern Venezuela. It also holds the record for the longest single drop of any waterfall—2,648 feet (807 m). As the upper river flows over the majestic cliffs, it takes 14 seconds for its water to plunge into the river below. Although rumors of this giant waterfall existed for many years, it was first documented by Ernesto Sanchez La Cruz in 1910. The falls were later named for an American bush pilot, Jimmy Angel, after he spotted them from the air.

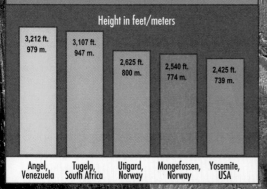

**THE WORLD'S HIGHEST WATERFALLS**

Height in feet/meters

| Angel, Venezuela | Tugela, South Africa | Utigard, Norway | Mongefossen, Norway | Yosemite, USA |
|---|---|---|---|---|
| 3,212 ft. 979 m. | 3,107 ft. 947 m. | 2,625 ft. 800 m. | 2,540 ft. 774 m. | 2,425 ft. 739 m. |

# World's Longest River

## The Nile

The Nile River in Africa flows for 4,145 miles (6,671 km) from the tributaries of Lake Victoria in Tanzania and Uganda out to the Mediterranean Sea. Because of varying depths, boats can sail on only about 2,000 miles (3,217 km) of the river. The Nile stretches through Rwanda, Uganda, Sudan, and Egypt. The river's water supply is crucial to the existence of these African countries. The Nile's precious water is used to irrigate crops and to generate electricity. Many animals, including fish, snakes, turtles, crocodiles, lizards, and hippos also depend on the Nile for shelter and food.

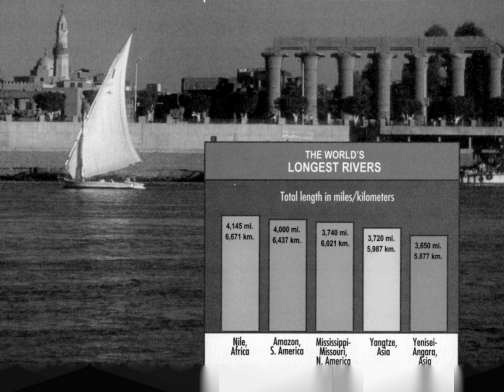

### THE WORLD'S LONGEST RIVERS

Total length in miles/kilometers

| Nile, Africa | Amazon, S. America | Mississippi-Missouri, N. America | Yangtze, Asia | Yenisei-Angara, Asia |
|---|---|---|---|---|
| 4,145 mi. 6,671 km. | 4,000 mi. 6,437 km. | 3,740 mi. 6,021 km. | 3,720 mi. 5,987 km. | 3,650 mi. 5.877 km. |

# World's
# Largest Rock

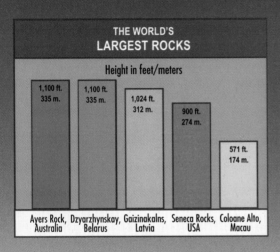

**THE WORLD'S LARGEST ROCKS**

Height in feet/meters

| Ayers Rock, Australia | Dzyarzhynskay, Belarus | Gaizinakalns, Latvia | Seneca Rocks, USA | Coloane Alto, Macau |
|---|---|---|---|---|
| 1,100 ft. 335 m. | 1,100 ft. 335 m. | 1,024 ft. 312 m. | 900 ft. 274 m. | 571 ft. 174 m. |

Located in the southwestern section of the Northern Territory of Australia, Ayers Rock shoots up 1,100 feet (335 m) above the surrounding desert. The oval-shaped rock is 2.2 miles (3.5 km) long and 1.5 miles (2.4 km) wide. Although it is not the tallest rock, Ayers Rock is the largest by volume. Ayers Rock is officially owned by Australia's native people, the Aborigines, who consider the caves at its base to be sacred. The Aborigines lease the giant monolith to the national government so the public may visit it as part of Uluru National Park.

## Ayers Rock

# World's
# Largest Island

# Greenland

Greenland, located in the North Atlantic Ocean, covers more than 840,000 square miles (2,175,600 sq km). Its jagged coastline is approximately 24,400 miles (39,267 km) long—about the same distance as Earth's circumference at the equator. From north to south, the island stretches for about 1,660 miles (2,670 km). About two-thirds of Greenland is located within the Arctic Circle. About 700,000 square miles (1,813,000 sq km) of this massive island are covered by a giant ice sheet that averages more than 5,000 feet (1,524 m) thick.

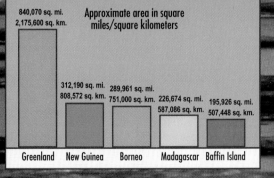

THE WORLD'S
**LARGEST ISLANDS**

Approximate area in square miles/square kilometers

| | | | | |
|---|---|---|---|---|
| 840,070 sq. mi. 2,175,600 sq. km. | 312,190 sq. mi. 808,572 sq. km. | 289,961 sq. mi. 751,000 sq. km. | 226,674 sq. mi. 587,086 sq. km. | 195,926 sq. mi. 507,448 sq. km. |
| Greenland | New Guinea | Borneo | Madagascar | Baffin Island |

**65**

# World's Deepest
# Sea Trench

## Mariana Trench

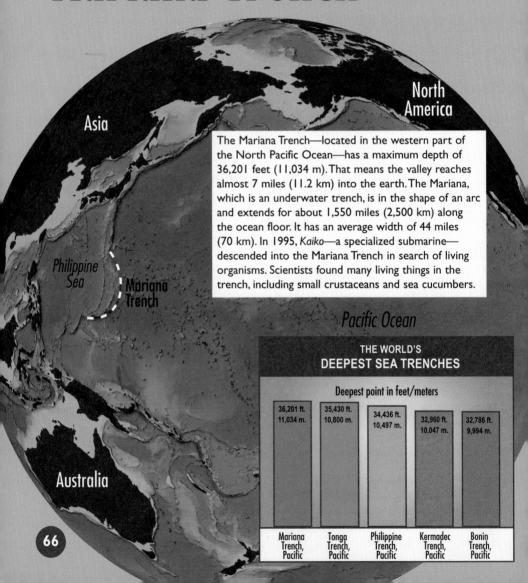

Asia

North America

Philippine Sea

Mariana Trench

Pacific Ocean

Australia

The Mariana Trench—located in the western part of the North Pacific Ocean—has a maximum depth of 36,201 feet (11,034 m). That means the valley reaches almost 7 miles (11.2 km) into the earth. The Mariana, which is an underwater trench, is in the shape of an arc and extends for about 1,550 miles (2,500 km) along the ocean floor. It has an average width of 44 miles (70 km). In 1995, *Kaiko*—a specialized submarine—descended into the Mariana Trench in search of living organisms. Scientists found many living things in the trench, including small crustaceans and sea cucumbers.

### THE WORLD'S DEEPEST SEA TRENCHES

#### Deepest point in feet/meters

| Mariana Trench, Pacific | Tonga Trench, Pacific | Philippine Trench, Pacific | Kermadec Trench, Pacific | Bonin Trench, Pacific |
|---|---|---|---|---|
| 36,201 ft. 11,034 m. | 35,430 ft. 10,800 m. | 34,436 ft. 10,497 m. | 32,960 ft. 10,047 m. | 32,786 ft. 9,994 m. |

# World's Most-Harvested Plant

## Corn

Corn is one of the world's most versatile plants. It is used to make oils, flours, meals, and is the basis for many livestock feeds. It is also sold and eaten fresh on the cob, cut and canned, frozen, or freeze-dried. Corn husks and silk are used around the world as part of shelters, clothing, and various decorations. All together, more than 662 million tons (600 t) of corn are produced around the world each year. China—the top producer—harvests about 21% of that total, with average annual production around 141 million tons (128 t).

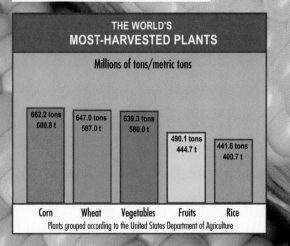

### THE WORLD'S MOST-HARVESTED PLANTS

Millions of tons/metric tons

| Corn | Wheat | Vegetables | Fruits | Rice |
|------|-------|------------|--------|------|
| 662.2 tons 600.8 t | 647.0 tons 587.0 t | 639.3 tons 580.0 t | 490.1 tons 444.7 t | 441.6 tons 400.7 t |

Plants grouped according to the United States Department of Agriculture

# World's
# Largest Seed

## Coco de Mer

The giant, dark brown seed of the coco de mer palm tree can reach 12 inches (30 cm) long, measure 3 feet (1 m) in diameter, and weigh up to 40 pounds (18 kg). The tree can grow up to 100 feet (31 m) tall, with leaves measuring 20 feet (6 m) long and 12 feet (3.6 m) wide. Coco de mer trees are found on the island of Praslin in the Seychelles Archipelago of the Indian Ocean. The area where some of the few remaining trees grow has been declared a Natural World Heritage Site in an effort to protect the species from poachers looking for the rare seeds. Only a few thousand seeds are produced each year.

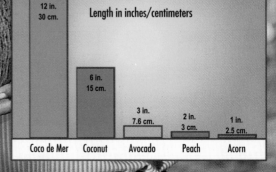

### SOME OF THE WORLD'S LARGEST SEEDS

Length in inches/centimeters

| Coco de Mer | Coconut | Avocado | Peach | Acorn |
|---|---|---|---|---|
| 12 in. 30 cm. | 6 in. 15 cm. | 3 in. 7.6 cm. | 2 in. 3 cm. | 1 in. 2.5 cm. |

# World's Oldest Living Tree

## Bristlecone Pine

In the Ancient Bristlecone Pine Forest, located in the White Mountains of California, lives a bristlecone pine tree that is estimated to be more than 4,700 years old. Nicknamed Methuselah, this tree is almost twice as old as the great pyramids of Egypt. Bristlecones are found in the western United States. They can grow as high as 60 feet (18.3 m) and some have a twisted, gnarly appearance.

### SOME OF THE WORLD'S OLDEST LIVING TREES

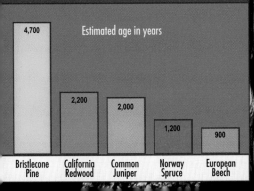

Estimated age in years

| Bristlecone Pine | California Redwood | Common Juniper | Norway Spruce | European Beech |
|---|---|---|---|---|
| 4,700 | 2,200 | 2,000 | 1,200 | 900 |

# World's Largest Flower

## Rafflesia

The giant rafflesia, also known as the "stinking corpse lily," has blossoms that can reach 3 feet (1 m) in diameter and weigh up to 25 pounds (11 kg). This endangered plant is found only in the rain forests of Borneo and Sumatra. It lives inside the bark of host vines, and is noticeable only when its flowers break through to blossom. The large, reddish-purple flowers remain open for about a week. They give off a smell similar to rotting meat, which attracts flies, beetles, and other flying insects. These insects

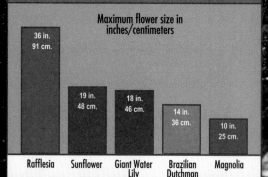

### THE WORLD'S LARGEST FLOWERS

Maximum flower size in inches/centimeters

| Flower | Size |
|---|---|
| Rafflesia | 36 in. 91 cm. |
| Sunflower | 19 in. 48 cm. |
| Giant Water Lily | 18 in. 46 cm. |
| Brazilian Dutchman | 14 in. 36 cm. |
| Magnolia | 10 in. 25 cm. |

# World's Deadliest Plant

## Castor Bean Plant

The seeds of the castor bean plant contain a protein called ricin. Scientists estimate that ricin is about 6,000 times more poisonous than cyanide and 12,000 times more poisonous than rattlesnake venom. It would take a particle of ricin only about the size of a grain of sand to kill a 160-pound (73-kg) adult. Amazingly, this same plant is used to produce castor oil, which is a valuable medicine. By using heat, scientists can separate the useful oil from the seed and leave the ricin behind. Castor bean plants grow in warmer climates and can reach a height of about 10 feet (3 m).

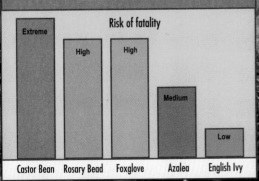

**THE WORLD'S DEADLIEST PLANTS**

Risk of fatality

| Castor Bean | Rosary Bead | Foxglove | Azalea | English Ivy |
|-------------|-------------|----------|--------|-------------|
| Extreme | High | High | Medium | Low |

# World's Fastest-Growing Land Plant

## Bamboo

Some species of bamboo can grow up to 1 foot (30 cm) a day. That means these plants are growing at a rate of about .5 inches (1.27 cm) every hour. Bamboo—which is actually a member of the grass family—has woody, hollow stems and thin leaves. Although it is found in many tropical and subtropical climates, most of the world's bamboo grows in East and Southeast Asia. It can range in height from 6 inches (15 cm) to 130 feet (40 m). Bamboo is also the sole food source for the world's most endangered animals, pandas.

### THE WORLD'S FASTEST-GROWING LAND PLANTS

Average growth per day in inches/centimeters

| Bamboo | Albizzia Falcata | Castor Bean Plant | Sunflower | Green bean |
|--------|------------------|-------------------|-----------|------------|
| 12 in. 30.4 cm. | 10 in. 25.4 cm. | 2 in. 5.1 cm. | 1 in. 2.5 cm. | .5 in. 1.3 cm. |

# World's Most
# Poisonous Mushroom

Estimates of the number of poisonous mushroom species range from 80 to 2,000. Most experts agree, however, that at least 100 varieties will cause severe symptoms and even death if eaten. Among the most dangerous mushrooms are members of the Amanita family, which includes Destroying Angels and the highly dangerous *Amanita phalloides*, or Death Cap. The Death Cap contains deadly peptide toxins that cause rapid loss of bodily fluids and intense thirst. Within six hours, the poison shuts down the kidneys, liver, and central nervous system, causing coma and—in more than 50% of cases—death.

## Death Cap

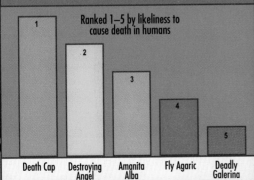

**THE WORLD'S MOST POISONOUS MUSHROOMS**

Ranked 1–5 by likeliness to cause death in humans

1. Death Cap
2. Destroying Angel
3. Amanita Alba
4. Fly Agaric
5. Deadly Galerina

# World's Tallest Cactus

## Saguaro

Although most saguaro cacti grow to a height of 50 feet (15 m), some have actually reached 75 feet (23 m). That's taller than a seven-story building. Saguaros start out quite small, and grow very slowly. A saguaro only reaches about 1 inch (2.5 cm) high during its first 10 years. It then grows about 4 inches (10 cm) a year. It will not bloom until it is between 50 and 75 years old. By this time, the cactus has a strong root system that can support about 9 to 10 tons (8 to 9 t) of growth. A saguaro may live for 150 to 200 years.

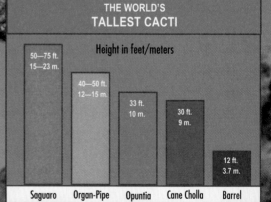

THE WORLD'S
TALLEST CACTI

Height in feet/meters

| Saguaro | Organ-Pipe | Opuntia | Cane Cholla | Barrel |
|---------|-----------|---------|-------------|--------|
| 50—75 ft. 15—23 m. | 40—50 ft. 12—15 m. | 33 ft. 10 m. | 30 ft. 9 m. | 12 ft. 3.7 m. |

# World's Largest Leaves

## Raffia Palm

The leaves of this tropical palm tree can reach lengths of 65 feet (19.8 m) long. That's about the same length as a regulation tennis court. Raffia trees are native to Madagascar, but can also be found along Africa's eastern coast. These enormous plants have several stems that can reach heights of 6 to 30 feet (2 to 9 m). When they reach about 50 years of age, raffia palms flower and produce egg-sized fruits covered in hard scales. Several products come from these palms, including raffia and floor and shoe polish. Raffia leaves are also used to weave baskets, mats, and hats.

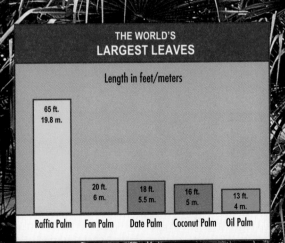

### THE WORLD'S LARGEST LEAVES

Length in feet/meters

| | | | | |
|---|---|---|---|---|
| 65 ft. 19.8 m. | 20 ft. 6 m. | 18 ft. 5.5 m. | 16 ft. 5 m. | 13 ft. 4 m. |
| Raffia Palm | Fan Palm | Date Palm | Coconut Palm | Oil Palm |

75

# World's
# Tallest Tree

## California Redwood

California redwoods, which grow in both California and southern Oregon, can reach 385 feet (117.35 m) in height. Their trunks can grow up to 25 feet (7.6 m) in diameter. The tallest recorded redwood stands 385 feet (117.35 m) tall—more than 60 feet (18.3 m) taller than the Statue of Liberty. Some redwoods are believed to be more than 2,000 years old. In the United States, redwoods are protected. Throughout the world, they are still destroyed by the timber industry and are near extinction.

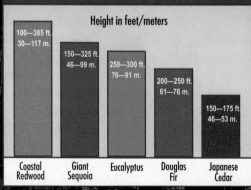

**THE WORLD'S TALLEST TREE SPECIES**

Height in feet/meters

| | | | | |
|---|---|---|---|---|
| 100—385 ft. 30—117 m. | | | | |
| | 150—325 ft. 46—99 m. | 250—300 ft. 76—91 m. | 200—250 ft. 61—76 m. | 150—175 ft. 46—53 m. |
| Coastal Redwood | Giant Sequoia | Eucalyptus | Douglas Fir | Japanese Cedar |

# World's Most Massive Tree

## Giant Sequoia

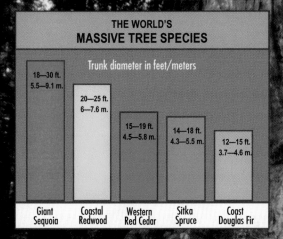

**THE WORLD'S MASSIVE TREE SPECIES**

Trunk diameter in feet/meters

- Giant Sequoia: 18—30 ft. 5.5—9.1 m.
- Coastal Redwood: 20—25 ft. 6—7.6 m.
- Western Red Cedar: 15—19 ft. 4.5—5.8 m.
- Sitka Spruce: 14—18 ft. 4.3—5.5 m.
- Coast Douglas Fir: 12—15 ft. 3.7—4.6 m.

Giant sequoias can grow between 150 and 325 feet (46 to 99 m) tall, with trunks measuring up to 30 feet (9 m) in diameter. They grow only in California, on the slopes of the Sierra-Nevada Mountains. General Sherman, the largest known living sequoia in the world, is 272 feet (83 m) tall. Its trunk measures 35 feet (10.6 m) in diameter, has a circumference of 109 feet (33 m) at the base, and weighs in at about 1,400 tons (1,270 t). That's the same weight as 25 military tanks! General Sherman also has an estimated 600,000 board feet (182,880 board m) of timber—enough to build more than 115 houses.

# World's Driest Inhabited Place

## Aswan

Aswan—Egypt's sunniest and southernmost city—receives an average rainfall of only .02 inches (.5 mm) per year. Summer temperatures can reach a blistering 114° Fahrenheit (46° C). Aswan is located on the west bank of the Nile River. The Aswan High Dam, at 12,565 feet (3,830 m) long, is the city's most famous landmark. It produces the majority of Egypt's power in the form of hydroelectricity. Aswan also has many Pharaonic, Greco-Roman, and Islamic ruins.

### THE WORLD'S DRIEST INHABITED PLACES

Average annual rainfall in inches/millimeters

| Aswan, Egypt | Luxor, Egypt | Arica, Chile | Ica, Peru | Antofagasta, Chile |
|---|---|---|---|---|
| 0.02 in. 0.50 mm. | 0.03 in. 0.76 mm. | 0.04 in. 1.0 mm. | 0.09 in. 2.3 mm. | 0.19 in. 4.8 mm. |

# World's Wettest
# Inhabited Place

## Buenaventura

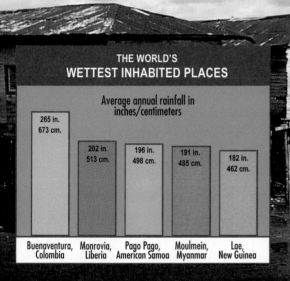

### THE WORLD'S WETTEST INHABITED PLACES

Average annual rainfall in inches/centimeters

| 265 in. 673 cm. | 202 in. 513 cm. | 196 in. 498 cm. | 191 in. 485 cm. | 182 in. 462 cm. |
|---|---|---|---|---|
| Buenaventura, Colombia | Monrovia, Liberia | Pago Pago, American Samoa | Moulmein, Myanmar | Lae, New Guinea |

Buenaventura, located near the thick South American jungles on the Pacific coast of Colombia, receives an average rainfall of 265 inches (673 cm) each year. That depth is equivalent to the height of a 22-story building. This city is best known for its shipping—it is home to Colombia's most important Pacific port. Each year, the port of Buenaventura receives corn, wheat, fertilizers, vehicles, and many other important goods. It also ships out many of Colombia's major agricultural products, including coffee, sugar, and molasses.

# World's Hottest Inhabited Place

## Djibouti

| THE WORLD'S HOTTEST INHABITED PLACES | | | | |
| --- | --- | --- | --- | --- |
| Average temperature in degrees Fahrenheit/Celsius | | | | |
| 86.0° F 30.0° C | 84.7° F 29.3° C | 84.7° F 29.3° C | 84.7° F 29.3° C | 84.6° F 29.2° C |
| Djibouti, Rep. of Djibouti | Timbuktu, Mali | Tirunelevi, India | Tuticorin, India | Nellore, India |

This port city is the capital of the Republic of Djibouti, which is located on the continent of Africa. During the hottest months, which are May through September, the monthly average temperature can reach 99° Fahrenheit (37° C). Even in the cool season, temperatures may reach above 85° Fahrenheit (30° C). Djibouti's climate is very dry, and few plant species survive there. There is little rainfall, and there are no surface rivers or streams that flow year-round. Most of the nation's water is supplied by the Houmbouli River, which flows underground.

# World's Coldest Inhabited Place

## Norilsk

Norilsk is a small city located in the Rybnaya Valley of central Russia. It is not surprising that the city's population has remained small—about 170,000 residents—because Norilsk has an average temperature of only 12.4° Fahrenheit (-10.9° C). That's an average of 20° Fahrenheit (-6.6° C) below freezing. Norilsk is north of the Arctic Circle, which accounts for its many days of freezing weather. The city also experiences five months without sunlight because of its polar location.

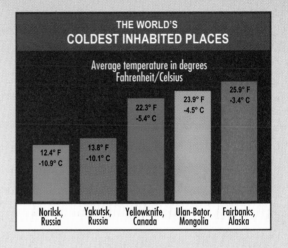

**THE WORLD'S COLDEST INHABITED PLACES**

Average temperature in degrees Fahrenheit/Celsius

| Norilsk, Russia | Yakutsk, Russia | Yellowknife, Canada | Ulan-Bator, Mongolia | Fairbanks, Alaska |
|---|---|---|---|---|
| 12.4° F -10.9° C | 13.8° F -10.1° C | 22.3° F -5.4° C | 23.9° F -4.5° C | 25.9° F -3.4° C |

# World's Greatest Snowfall

## Mount Rainier

Between 1971 and 1972, Mount Rainier had a record snowfall of 1,224 inches (3,109 cm). That's enough snow to cover a 10-story building! Located in the Cascade Mountains of Washington state, Mount Rainier is a dormant volcano that last erupted about 2,000 years ago. The mountain, which covers about 100 square miles (260 sq km), reaches a height of 14,410 feet (4,392 m). Its three peaks include Liberty Cap, Point Success, and Columbia Crest.

### THE WORLD'S GREATEST ANNUAL SNOWFALLS

Highest annual snowfall in inches/centimeters

| Mount Rainier, Washington, 1971–1972 | Mount Baker, Washington, 1998–1999 | Paradise Station, Washington, 1971–1972 | Thompson Pass, Alaska, 1952–1953 | Mount Copeland, British Columbia, 1971–1972 |
|---|---|---|---|---|
| 1,224 in. 3,109 cm. | 1,140 in. 2,895 cm. | 1,122 in. 2,849 cm. | 974 in. 2,474 cm. | 964 in. 2,449 cm. |

# Place with the World's Fastest Winds

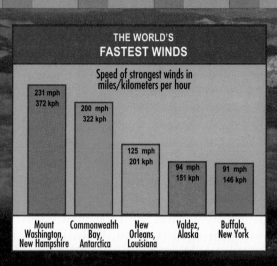

**THE WORLD'S FASTEST WINDS**

Speed of strongest winds in miles/kilometers per hour

| Mount Washington, New Hampshire | Commonwealth Bay, Antarctica | New Orleans, Louisiana | Valdez, Alaska | Buffalo, New York |
|---|---|---|---|---|
| 231 mph 372 kph | 200 mph 322 kph | 125 mph 201 kph | 94 mph 151 kph | 91 mph 146 kph |

Even though the average wind speed at the summit of Mount Washington is approximately 36 miles (58 km) per hour, winds often whip by this mountain at much higher speeds. In 1934, winds reached a world record of 231 miles (372 km) per hour—and these gusts were not part of a storm. Located in the White Mountains of New Hampshire, Mount Washington is the highest peak in New England at 6,288 feet (1,917 m). The treeless summit, which is known for its harsh weather, has an average annual temperature of only 26.5° Fahrenheit (-3.1° C).

# Mount Washington

# Human-Made Records

**Bridges • Constructions • Dams
Transportation • Travel • Tunnels**

# World's Highest Bridge

## Royal Gorge

### THE WORLD'S HIGHEST BRIDGES

Height in feet/meters

| | | | | |
|---|---|---|---|---|
| 1,053 ft. 321 m. | 228 ft. 69 m. | 203 ft. 62 m. | 133 ft. 41 m. | 89 ft. 27 m. |
| Royal Gorge, USA | Verrazano-Narrows, USA | Tsing Ma, China | Brooklyn, USA | Banghwa Grand, N. Korea |

The Royal Gorge Bridge—in Canon City, Colorado—spans the Arkansas River 1,053 feet (321 m) above the water. Built in 1929, the bridge is 1,260 feet (384 m) long and 18 feet (5 m) wide. About 1,000 tons (247 t) of steel make up the bridge's floor, which can hold in excess of 2 million pounds (907,200 kg). The cables weigh about 300 tons (272 t) each.

# World's Longest
# Suspension Bridge

## Akashi-Kaikyo

Built in 1998, this giant suspension bridge connects Maiko, Tarumi Ward, in Kobe City to Matsuho, Awaji Town, in Tsuna County on the Japanese island of Awajishima. All together, the bridge spans the Akashi Strait for 2 miles (3219 m). The structure's main span is a record-breaking 6,529 feet (1,990 m) long, and the main tower soars approximately 984 feet (300 m) into the air. Each main cable measures 3.5 feet (1 m) in diameter—the total length of wire used in just one main cable is 186,420 miles (300,005 km).

### THE WORLD'S
### LONGEST SUSPENSION BRIDGES

Length of main span in feet/meters

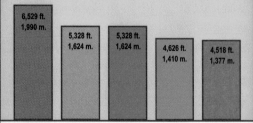

| | | | | |
|---|---|---|---|---|
| 6,529 ft. 1,990 m. | 5,328 ft. 1,624 m. | 5,328 ft. 1,624 m. | 4,626 ft. 1,410 m. | 4,518 ft. 1,377 m. |
| Akashi-Kaikyo, Japan | Great Belt, Denmark | Jiangyin, China | Humber Estuary, UK | Tsing Ma, China |

# World's Largest Stadium

## Strahov Stadium

The Strahov Stadium, located in Prague, Czech Republic, can seat up to 240,000 people. That's roughly the same size as the entire population of Raleigh, North Carolina. The stadium was completed in 1934 for the Sokol gymnastics exhibition. Today, the facility is used for Spartakiadas, which are large gymnastic shows. The stadium also hosts a variety of other sporting events and cultural programs. In comparison, the United States' largest stadium—located at the University of Michigan—has less than one-half the seating capacity of Strahov Stadium.

### THE WORLD'S LARGEST SPORTS STADIUMS

Seating capacity

| Stadium | Seating capacity |
|---|---|
| Strahov, Czech Republic | 240,000 |
| Maracana, Brazil | 205,000 |
| Rungnado, North Korea | 150,000 |
| Maghalaes Pinto, Brazil | 125,000 |
| Morumbi, Brazil | 120,000 |

# World's Tallest Habitable Building

## Petronas Towers

Each of these giant, identical skyscrapers is 1,483 feet (452 m) tall. They soar above the city of Kuala Lumpur in Malaysia and contain the headquarters for Petronas, the country's national petroleum company. The two 88-story towers are circular, with a 191-foot- (58-m) long sky bridge that connects them at the forty-first and forty-second floors. The buildings cover approximately 3.7 million square feet (343,730 sq m) and contain 36,910 tons (33,84 t) of beams and reinforcements. Each of the towers has 29 high-speed elevators and 10 escalators, along with miles (kilometers) of wiring and cable.

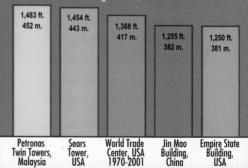

### THE WORLD'S TALLEST HABITABLE BUILDINGS

**Height in feet/meters**

| Petronas Twin Towers, Malaysia | Sears Tower, USA | World Trade Center, USA 1970-2001 | Jin Mao Building, China | Empire State Building, USA |
|---|---|---|---|---|
| 1,483 ft. 452 m. | 1,454 ft. 443 m. | 1,368 ft. 417 m. | 1,255 ft. 382 m. | 1,250 ft. 381 m. |

# City with the Most Skyscrapers

## New York City

New York City, at the mouth of the Hudson River in southeastern New York State, is an area more than 308 square miles (797 sq km). It has more than 140 skyscrapers towering over its streets. A solid platform of bedrock has made it possible for the island to support such large structures. Manhattan's buildings come in almost every shape and size and represent every major architectural style from the nineteenth century to the present. Some of the city's tallest skyscrapers—such as the Empire State Building and the Chrysler Building—are world famous.

### WORLD CITIES WITH THE MOST SKYSCRAPERS

Number of skyscrapers

| City | Number |
| --- | --- |
| New York City, New York | 140 |
| Chicago, Illinois | 68 |
| Hong Kong, China | 36 |
| Houston, Texas | 36 |
| Kuala Lumpur, Malaysia | 25 |

89

# World's Tallest
# Free-Standing Tower

## CN Tower

Located in Toronto, Canada, the Canadian National Tower reaches a height of 1,815 feet (553 m). It was built both to demonstrate the strength of Canadian industry and to solve some of the city's communications problems. In the 1960s, Toronto businesses built several tall buildings that interfered with electronic transmission and reception. The CN Tower's 1,109-foot- (338-m) high microwave receptors and roof antenna solved these problems. Each year, about 2 million people visit the tower and take in the view from the highest observation deck in the world.

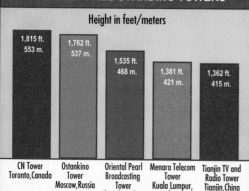

**THE WORLD'S
TALLEST FREE-STANDING TOWERS**

Height in feet/meters

|  |  |
|---|---|
| CN Tower Toronto, Canada | 1,815 ft. 553 m. |
| Ostankino Tower Moscow, Russia | 1,762 ft. 537 m. |
| Oriental Pearl Broadcasting Tower Shanghai, China | 1,535 ft. 468 m. |
| Menara Telecom Tower Kuala Lumpur, Malaysia | 1,381 ft. 421 m. |
| Tianjin TV and Radio Tower Tianjin, China | 1,362 ft. 415 m. |

# World's
# Largest Mall

West Edmonton Mall

## THE WORLD'S LARGEST MALLS

Area in millions of
square feet /square meters

| West Edmonton Mall, Canada | Mall of America, USA | Sawgrass Mills Mall, USA | Austin Mall, Texas | Suntec City Mall, Singapore |
|---|---|---|---|---|
| 5.3 M sq. ft. .49 M sq. m. | 4.2 M sq. ft. .39 M sq. m. | 2.3 M sq. ft. .21 M sq. m. | 1.1 M sq. ft. .10 M sq. m. | .89 M sq. ft. .08 M sq. m. |

The West Edmonton Mall—located in Alberta, Canada—occupies a total of 5.3 million square feet (.49 million sq m). This giant shopping and entertainment complex features more than 800 stores and services. Popular restaurants like the Hard Rock Cafe and the Rainforest Cafe® are also located there. In addition to stores and eateries, the West Edmonton Mall also houses an amusement park, the world's largest indoor lake with four working submarines, an NHL-sized ice arena, 26 movie theaters, dolphin shows, a casino, and a miniature golf course.

# World's Largest
# Amusement Park

## Walt Disney World Resort

The Walt Disney World Resort in Lake Buena Vista, Florida, opened in 1971 and covers more than 30,000 acres (12,141 ha). Given its size, the resort is more like a small town than an amusement park. The majority of the complex is made up of hotels and giant theme parks, including the Magic Kingdom, Disney's Animal Kingdom, Epcot, and Disney-MGM Studios. There are also several water parks, shopping areas, movie theaters, and sports complexes. This giant resort even has its own fire station and transportation department!

## SOME OF THE WORLD'S LARGEST AMUSEMENT PARKS

Size in acres/hectares

| Walt Disney World Resort, USA | Great Adventure, USA | Cedar Point, USA | Busch Gardens, USA | Tokyo Disney Resort, Japan |
|---|---|---|---|---|
| 30,000 ac. 12,141 ha. | 620 ac. 251 ha. | 364 ac. 147 ha. | 335 ac. 135 ha. | 114 ac. 46 ha. |

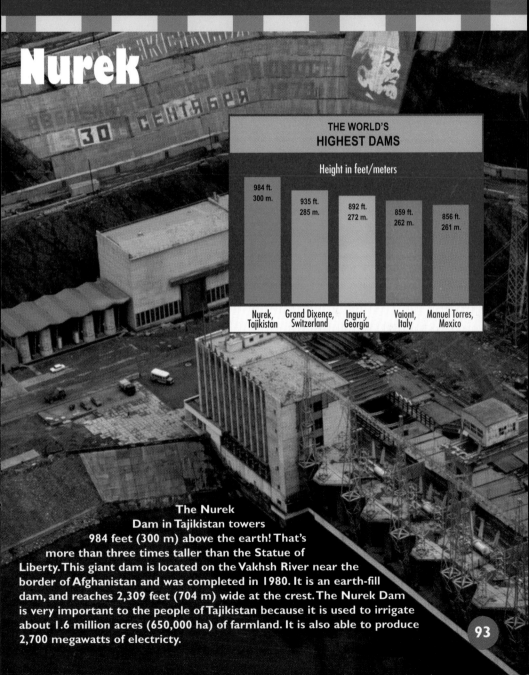

# World's Highest Dam

## Nurek

### THE WORLD'S HIGHEST DAMS

Height in feet/meters

| Nurek, Tajikistan | Grand Dixence, Switzerland | Inguri, Georgia | Vaiont, Italy | Manuel Torres, Mexico |
|---|---|---|---|---|
| 984 ft. 300 m. | 935 ft. 285 m. | 892 ft. 272 m. | 859 ft. 262 m. | 856 ft. 261 m. |

The Nurek Dam in Tajikistan towers 984 feet (300 m) above the earth! That's more than three times taller than the Statue of Liberty. This giant dam is located on the Vakhsh River near the border of Afghanistan and was completed in 1980. It is an earth-fill dam, and reaches 2,309 feet (704 m) wide at the crest. The Nurek Dam is very important to the people of Tajikistan because it is used to irrigate about 1.6 million acres (650,000 ha) of farmland. It is also able to produce 2,700 megawatts of electricty.

# World's
# Largest Reservoir

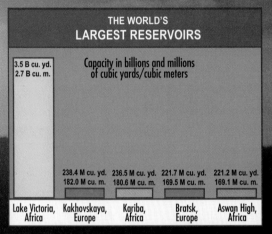

**THE WORLD'S
LARGEST RESERVOIRS**

| | | | | |
|---|---|---|---|---|
| **3.5 B cu. yd.**<br>**2.7 B cu. m.** | Capacity in billions and millions<br>of cubic yards/cubic meters | | | |
| | 238.4 M cu. yd.<br>182.0 M cu. m. | 236.5 M cu. yd.<br>180.6 M cu. m. | 221.7 M cu. yd.<br>169.5 M cu. m. | 221.2 M cu. yd.<br>169.1 M cu. m. |
| Lake Victoria,<br>Africa | Kakhovskaya,<br>Europe | Kariba,<br>Africa | Bratsk,<br>Europe | Aswan High,<br>Africa |

The construction of the Owen Falls Dam in 1954 turned Lake Victoria into a giant reservoir, capable of holding 3.5 billion cubic yards (2.7 billion cu m) of water. Lake Victoria is located off the Victoria Nile. The lake is bordered by Uganda, Kenya, and Tanzania in central Africa. The reservoir has an area of 26,830 square miles (69,490 sq km) and reaches 150 miles (241 km) at its widest point. Lake Victoria stores water during high-flood years for use during dry years. The power of the waterfall is used as electricity for the heavily populated countries of Uganda and Kenya.

# Lake Victoria

# World's Longest
# Ship Canal

## St. Lawrence Seaway

This giant ship canal is almost 2,500 miles (4,023 km) long, stretching from Montreal, Canada, to Duluth, Minnesota. It connects the North River in the United States with the Cabot Strait in Canada. It allows ships to travel from Lake Superior out to the Atlantic Ocean. The St. Lawrence Seaway was completed in 1959 and is an important ship route between the agricultural and industrial centers of central North America and Europe. There are a total of 20 locks to raise and lower ships on the seaway. The seaway's width varies from 442 to 550 feet (134 to 167 m).

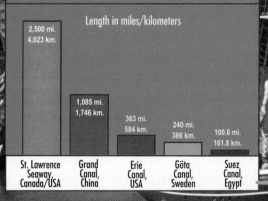

**THE WORLD'S LONGEST SHIP CANALS**

Length in miles/kilometers

| | | | | |
|---|---|---|---|---|
| 2,500 mi. 4,023 km. | 1,085 mi. 1,746 km. | 363 mi. 584 km. | 240 mi. 386 km. | 100.6 mi. 161.8 km. |
| St. Lawrence Seaway Canada/USA | Grand Canal, China | Erie Canal, USA | Göta Canal, Sweden | Suez Canal, Egypt |

# Country with the Most Bicycles

## The Netherlands

Per capita, the Netherlands has more bicycles than any other country, including China. There are an estimated 16 million bicycles in the Netherlands, which averages out to about one bike for every person in the country. Many people around the world—especially those in crowded cities—have realized that bicycling is an easy way to get around and a great way to cut down on pollution. The Netherlands, in particular, is battling a major pollution problem, and it is one of the world's most densely populated nations.

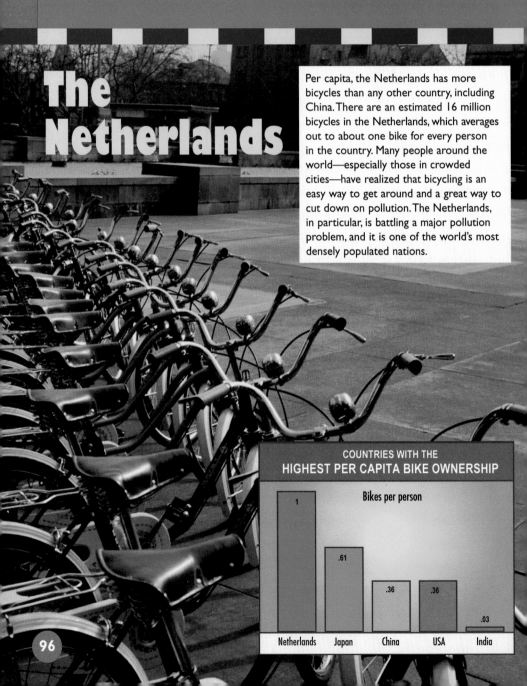

**COUNTRIES WITH THE HIGHEST PER CAPITA BIKE OWNERSHIP**

Bikes per person

| Netherlands | Japan | China | USA | India |
|---|---|---|---|---|
| 1 | .61 | .36 | .36 | .03 |

# Country with the Most Cars

## The United States

The citizens of the United States own 135 million automobiles. That's about 28% of all the automobiles owned in the world. It means that for every two Americans there is one car. That figure doesn't even include all of the trucks, campers, and motorcycles in the country. Almost 90% of all U.S. residents have access to motor vehicles. With 15 million cars, California has the most registered automobiles in the nation. Because 88% of Americans drive their vehicles to work, the United States has severe traffic problems. During peak rush hours, about 70% of interstate highways are heavily congested.

**COUNTRIES WITH THE MOST CARS**

Number of cars, in millions

| USA | Japan | Germany | Italy | France |
|-----|-------|---------|-------|--------|
| 135 M | 44.6 M | 40.5 M | 30 M | 25.1 M |

# Country with the Longest Rail Network

## The United States

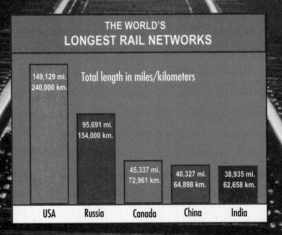

**THE WORLD'S LONGEST RAIL NETWORKS**

Total length in miles/kilometers

| USA | Russia | Canada | China | India |
|-----|--------|--------|-------|-------|
| 149,129 mi. 240,000 km. | 95,691 mi. 154,000 km. | 45,337 mi. 72,961 km. | 40,327 mi. 64,898 km. | 38,935 mi. 62,658 km. |

About 149,000 miles (240,000 km) of railroad track spans America, connecting all of the 48 continental states. That's enough track to circle the Earth five times. Today, five railways carry about 40% of the nation's intercity freight, 65% of its coal, and 40% of its grain. In the last year, locomotives hauled a total of 1.38 ton-miles (2.2 km) of freight. There are 20,261 locomotives and 1.3 million freight cars in operation today. It would take 3 million trucks to equal the capacity of the U.S. rail car fleet.

# City with the
# Busiest Subway System

## Moscow

Each year, approximately 3.18 billion people ride on Moscow's bustling Metropolitan (Metro) subway system. It is not only busy, it is also world renowned for its beautiful architecture. Many of the 150 stations have stained glass, marble statuary, and sparkling chandeliers. The rail network is 153 miles (246 km) long and follows the street pattern above. The subways are gradually being extended to reach the many commuters who live on the outskirts of the city. On average, Muscovites spend about two hours commuting each day.

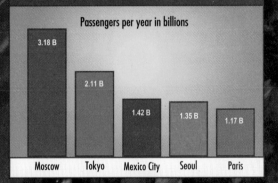

THE WORLD'S BUSIEST
**SUBWAY SYSTEMS**

Passengers per year in billions

| Moscow | Tokyo | Mexico City | Seoul | Paris |
|--------|-------|-------------|-------|-------|
| 3.18 B | 2.11 B | 1.42 B | 1.35 B | 1.17 B |

# World's
# Busiest Airport

## Hartsfield Atlanta International

In one year, an average of more than 78 million passengers travel through the Hartsfield Atlanta International Airport. That's more people than are living in California, Texas, and Florida combined. Approximately 2,080 planes depart and arrive at this airport every day. With parking lots, runways, maintenance facilities, and other buildings, the Hartsfield terminal complex covers about 130 acres (53 ha). The airport employs almost 34,000 people, making it the largest single employment center in Georgia.

### THE WORLD'S BUSIEST AIRPORTS

Annual passengers in millions

| Airport | Passengers |
|---|---|
| Hartsfield Atlanta Intl., USA | 78.1 M |
| Chicago O'Hare Intl., USA | 72.6 M |
| Los Angeles Intl., USA | 64.2 M |
| Heathrow Intl., England | 62.2 M |
| Dallas/Fort Worth Intl., USA | 60.0 M |

# Country with the
# Most Airports

## The United States

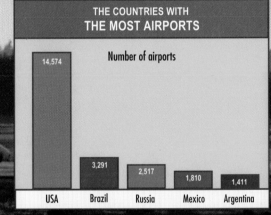

**THE COUNTRIES WITH THE MOST AIRPORTS**

Number of airports

| | | | | |
|---|---|---|---|---|
| 14,574 | 3,291 | 2,517 | 1,810 | 1,411 |
| USA | Brazil | Russia | Mexico | Argentina |

The United States leads the world with 14,574 airports. That is more than the number of airports for the other nine top countries combined. The top three busiest airports in the world are also located in the United States. All together, U.S. airports serve more than 635 million travelers a year. In 1999, the airline industry employed more than 1.2 million workers and operated just under 5,000 airplanes.

# World's Top
# Tourist Country

## France

Each year, more than 71 million tourists visit France. That's equal to the number of people living in all of California, Florida, and Texas combined. The most popular French destinations are Paris and the Mediterranean coast. In July and August—the most popular time to visit France—tourists flock to the westernmost coastal areas of the region. In the winter, visitors hit the slopes at some major ski resorts in the northern Alps. Most tourists are from other European countries, especially Germany. All of this business has a great effect on the economy—the French tourism industry employs about 7% of the country's total population.

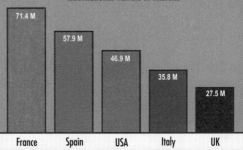

**THE WORLD'S TOP TOURIST COUNTRIES**

International visitors in millions

| France | Spain | USA | Italy | UK |
|--------|-------|-------|-------|-------|
| 71.4 M | 57.9 M | 46.9 M | 35.8 M | 27.5 M |

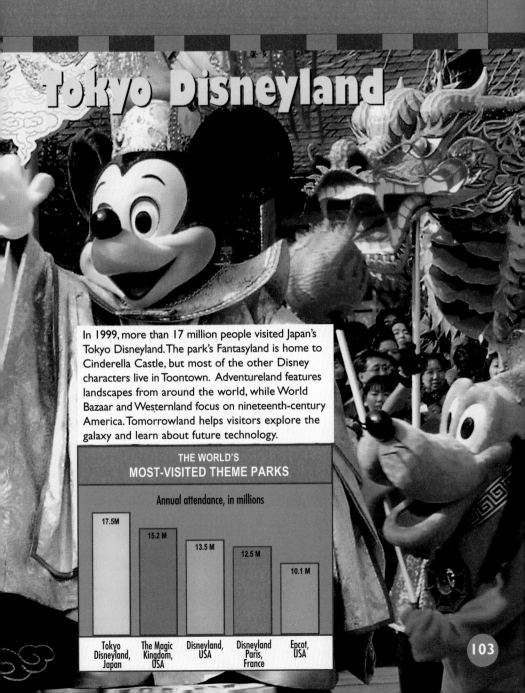

# World's Most-Visited Amusement Park

## Tokyo Disneyland

In 1999, more than 17 million people visited Japan's Tokyo Disneyland. The park's Fantasyland is home to Cinderella Castle, but most of the other Disney characters live in Toontown. Adventureland features landscapes from around the world, while World Bazaar and Westernland focus on nineteenth-century America. Tomorrowland helps visitors explore the galaxy and learn about future technology.

### THE WORLD'S MOST-VISITED THEME PARKS

Annual attendance, in millions

| Park | Attendance |
|------|-----------|
| Tokyo Disneyland, Japan | 17.5M |
| The Magic Kingdom, USA | 15.2 M |
| Disneyland, USA | 13.5 M |
| Disneyland Paris, France | 12.5 M |
| Epcot, USA | 10.1 M |

# World's
# Busiest Port

## Rotterdam

This enormous port, on the southwestern coast of the Netherlands, handles more than 385 million tons (349 million t) of goods per year. The most common cargo that moves through Rotterdam is crude oil, ore and scrap metal, and coal. In 1962, Rotterdam became the world's largest port. Today, approximately 30,000 ships travel its waters each year.

### THE WORLD'S TOP FIVE
### BUSIEST PORTS

Goods handled per year,
in million tons/million metric tons

| Rotterdam, Netherlands | Singapore | Chiba, Japan | Kobe, Japan | Hong Kong, China |
|---|---|---|---|---|
| 385,800 tons 349,000 t | 319,600 tons 289,000 t | 191,400 tons 173,000 t | 188,400 tons 170,000 t | 162,200 tons 147,000 t |

# World's Longest Road Tunnel

## St. Gotthard

The St. Gotthard Road Tunnel stretches for a total of 10 miles (16 km) between the cities of Goschenen, Switzerland, and Airolo, Italy. The tunnel is so large that it is able to accommodate up to 1,500 cars per hour. The tunnel is 25 feet (7.6 m) wide and 15 feet (4.6 m) high. One major reason the tunnel was built was to ease traffic congestion. At peak times, however, cars can be backed up in the tunnel for miles. Switzerland has a high rate of cars per capita, and the busy travel seasons bring in hundreds of thousands of extra vehicles daily.

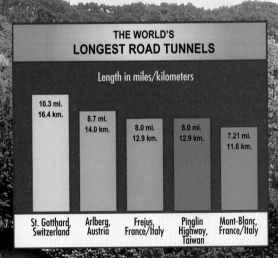

**THE WORLD'S LONGEST ROAD TUNNELS**

Length in miles/kilometers

| | Length in miles/kilometers | | | |
|---|---|---|---|---|
| 10.3 mi. 16.4 km. | 8.7 mi. 14.0 km. | 8.0 mi. 12.9 km. | 8.0 mi. 12.9 km. | 7.21 mi. 11.6 km. |
| St. Gotthard, Switzerland | Arlberg, Austria | Frejus, France/Italy | Pinglin Highway, Taiwan | Mont-Blanc, France/Italy |

# World's Longest Underwater Tunnel

The Seikan Tunnel connects Honshu—the main island of Japan—to Hokkaido, an island to the north. Stretching for a total of 33.4 miles (53.8 km), it is both the longest railway tunnel and underwater tunnel in the world. Some 14.3 miles (23 km) of the tunnel run under the Tsugaru Strait, which connects the Pacific Ocean to the Sea of Japan. A railway in the tunnel transports passengers. Construction began in 1964 and took 24 years to complete. Today, the Seikan Tunnel is no longer the quickest way between the two islands. Air travel is faster and is almost the same price.

THE WORLD'S
**LONGEST UNDERWATER TUNNELS**

Length in miles/kilometers

| Tunnel | Length |
| --- | --- |
| Seikan Tunnel, Japan | 33.4 mi. / 53.8 km. |
| Channel Tunnel, France/England | 31.0 mi. / 49.9 km. |
| Dai-Shimizu Tunnel, Japan | 13.8 mi. / 22.2 km. |
| Shin-Kanmom Tunnel, Japan | 11.6 mi. / 18.7 km. |
| Great Belt Link Tunnel, Denmark | 5.0 mi. / 8.0 km. |

# Seikan Tunnel

# U.S.
# Records

## Alabama to Wyoming

# State with the World's Largest
## Motorcycle Museum

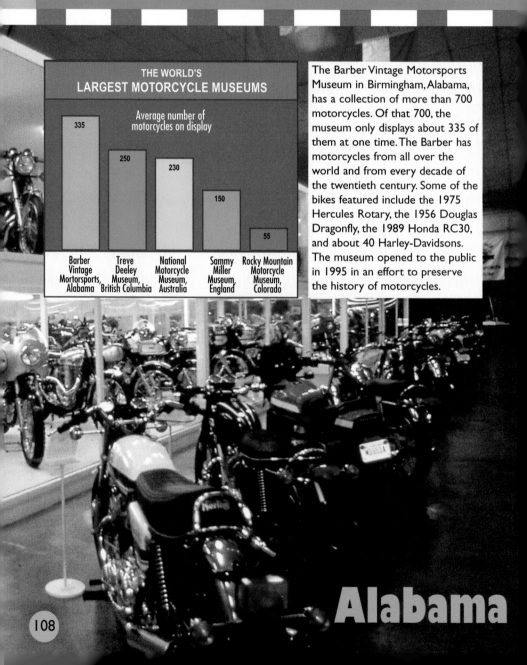

**THE WORLD'S LARGEST MOTORCYCLE MUSEUMS**

Average number of motorcycles on display

|  |  |
|---|---|
| Barber Vintage Mortorsports, Alabama | 335 |
| Treve Deeley Museum, British Columbia | 250 |
| National Motorcycle Museum, Australia | 230 |
| Sammy Miller Museum, England | 150 |
| Rocky Mountain Motorcycle Museum, Colorado | 55 |

The Barber Vintage Motorsports Museum in Birmingham, Alabama, has a collection of more than 700 motorcycles. Of that 700, the museum only displays about 335 of them at one time. The Barber has motorcycles from all over the world and from every decade of the twentieth century. Some of the bikes featured include the 1975 Hercules Rotary, the 1956 Douglas Dragonfly, the 1989 Honda RC30, and about 40 Harley-Davidsons. The museum opened to the public in 1995 in an effort to preserve the history of motorcycles.

# Alabama

# State with the Longest Shoreline

## Alaska

The tidal shoreline of Alaska wraps around three-fourths of the state, stretching for almost 34,000 miles (54,716 km). Another 6,600 miles (10,621 km) of coastline fronts the open sea. To the north and northwest of Alaska is the Arctic Ocean. To the west are the Bering Strait and the Bering Sea. The Pacific Ocean and the Gulf of Alaska meet the state's southern shoreline. Because of its location, it is not surprising that the fishing industry thrives in Alaska. In fact, the world's largest salmon-packing plant is located on Kodiak Island. Herring, cod, pollack, and halibut are also abundant in the surrounding waters.

### THE UNITED STATES' LONGEST SHORELINES

Shoreline in miles/kilometers

| Alaska | Florida | Louisiana | Maine | California |
|--------|---------|-----------|-------|-----------|
| 33,904 mi. 54,562 km. | 8,426 mi. 13,560 km. | 7,721 mi. 12,426 km. | 3,478 mi. 5,597 km. | 3,427 mi. 5,515 km. |

# State with the
# Most Tribal Land

## Arizona

### THE UNITED STATES'
### GREATEST AREAS OF TRIBAL LAND

Number of acres/hectacres,
in millions

| | | | | |
|---|---|---|---|---|
| 20.1 M ac. 8.1 M ha. | 7.9 M ac. 3.2 M ha. | 5.6 M ac. 2.3 M ha. | 4.5 M ac. 1.8 M ha. | 2.7 M ac. 1.1 M ha. |
| Arizona | New Mexico | Montana | South Dakota | Nevada |

The federal government has set aside 20.1 million acres of Arizona land to be used as Native American reservations. That's an area nearly equal to the entire state of Maine. About 5% of Arizona residents are of Native American descent, making them the largest Native American population in the United States. There are 15 Native American groups living on 17 reservations. The largest Native American groups living in Arizona are the Navajo, Hopi, Papago, and Pima. The Havasupai live at the bottom of the Grand Canyon. Human settlement in Arizona dates back almost 25,000 years to the Anasazi and the Hohokam.

# State with the Largest Retail Headquarters

## Arkansas

Wal-Mart—headquartered in Bentonville, Arkansas—logged more than $191.3 billion in sales in 2000. The company was founded in 1962 by Arkansas native Sam Walton, who saw his small variety stores grow into giant grocery stores, membership warehouse clubs, and deep-discount warehouse outlets. Through the years, Wal-Mart has created jobs for more than 6 million Americans. Walton's original store in Bentonville now serves as the company's visitor center.

**THE UNITED STATES' LARGEST RETAIL HEADQUARTERS**

Sales, in billions of dollars

| | | | | |
|---|---|---|---|---|
| $191.3 B | $45.7 B | $40.9 B | $37.0 B | $36.9 B |
| Wal-Mart, Arkansas | Home Depot, Georgia | Sears Roebuck, Illinois | Kmart, Michigan | Target, Minnesota |

# State with the
# Lowest Elevation

## California

Death Valley is located in southeastern California. At its deepest point, this valley reaches an incredible 282 feet (86 m) below sea level. Death Valley is about 140 miles (225 km) long and measures 15 miles wide in some areas. Altogether, about 550 square miles (1,425 sq km) of this national park lie below sea level. High temperatures and low rainfall make Death Valley a very arid environment. But despite these harsh conditions, many plants and animals thrive here. Cresote bush, pickleweed, and mesquite are all found here, as are bighorn sheep, rabbits, coyotes, and bobcats.

### AREAS OF THE UNITED STATES WITH THE LOWEST ELEVATIONS

Elevation at or below sea level in feet/meters

| Death Valley, California | New Orleans, Louisiana | Coastal Alabama | Coastal Florida | Coastal Maryland |
|---|---|---|---|---|
| -282 ft. -86 m. | -8 ft. -2 m. | 0 ft. 0 m. | 0 ft. 0 m. | 0 ft. 0 m. |

# State with the Highest Average Elevation

## Colorado

At an average of 6,800 feet (2,073 m) above sea level, Colorado is the nation's highest state. Its diverse landscape includes plains, rolling hills, plateaus, and mountain ranges. Between these areas, elevations range from 3,500 feet (1,067 m) to more than 14,000 feet (4,267 m). The highest point in the state is located in the central region of the Colorado Rockies. Mount Elbert, the highest peak in the Sawatch range, reaches a height of 14,433 feet (4,399 m). Besides Mount Elbert, there are more than 850 peaks that measure higher than 11,000 feet.

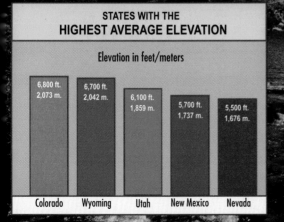

STATES WITH THE
HIGHEST AVERAGE ELEVATION

Elevation in feet/meters

| Colorado | Wyoming | Utah | New Mexico | Nevada |
|---|---|---|---|---|
| 6,800 ft. 2,073 m. | 6,700 ft. 2,042 m. | 6,100 ft. 1,859 m. | 5,700 ft. 1,737 m. | 5,500 ft. 1,676 m. |

# State with the Oldest Newspaper

# Connecticut

*The Hartford Courant*, which was started as a weekly paper in 1764 by Thomas Green, is actually older than the United States. In fact, George Washington placed an ad in the *Courant* to lease part of his Mount Vernon land. *The Hartford Courant* became a daily paper in 1837, and its Sunday edition began in 1913. The *Courant* has also won two Pulitzer Prizes during its more than 235 years: one for coverage of breaking news and one for explanatory journalism. Today, the newspaper has a circulation of more than 200,000 for dailies and 300,000 for the Sunday edition.

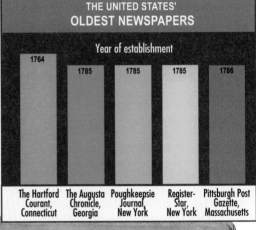

**THE UNITED STATES' OLDEST NEWSPAPERS**

Year of establishment

| The Hartford Courant, Connecticut | The Augusta Chronicle, Georgia | Poughkeepsie Journal, New York | Register-Star, New York | Pittsburgh Post Gazette, Massachusetts |
|---|---|---|---|---|
| 1764 | 1785 | 1785 | 1785 | 1786 |

## The Hartford Courant

Established 1764, Daily Edition, Vol. CLII No. 292    Thursday, October 19, 1989—8 Sections    Copyright 1989, The Hartford Courant Co. **30¢**

# Quake's devastation emerges

**Combined Wire Services**

SAN FRANCISCO — The devastation caused by the San Francisco Bay Area's catastrophic earthquake became clearer Wednesday, even as a sobering new reality began to set in: how long it will take to recover from the quake's stunning fury.

Tuesday's rush-hour quake of 6.9 on the Richter scale — the nation's second-deadliest and the worst since the Bay Area's disastrous quake of 1906 — made for a surreal scene as Wednesday dawned. Damage was everywhere.

Hundreds of small aftershocks — some of them noticeable, some of them not — continued to ripple along the San Andreas fault as Lt. Gov. Leo McCarthy put the death toll at 271 Wednesday morning. At least 1,400 were reported injured.

San Francisco Mayor Art Agnos estimated damages at $2 billion to public and private property in San Francisco city and county alone.

The full scope of the quake unfolded as officials made contact with hard-hit areas, where many telephones were cut off. As many as 1 million people were without power

**The aftermath**
- 271 people killed, 1,400 reported injured.
- Damage estimated at more than $1 billion.
- 1 million people left without power.

or other services, authorities reported.

This is just a devastating, terrible, terrible situation beyond everybody's imagination," said Marty Boyer, an Alameda County, Calif., spokesman.

Across San Francisco Bay in Oakland, some of the worst catastrophe and, scene of the worst catastrophe seven bodies had been pulled

under a mile-long stretch of elevated I-880 that had collapsed onto cars below.

Approximately 250 people were feared entombed in the wreckage, and ...were dead are.

assumed only one person per car.

An early report Wednesday that rescuers heard a voice coming from a car underneath the freeway's top level was dismissed as erroneous by police Capt. Jim Hahn.

mistake had been made. ..."garbled as been

worker helping to lift the slabs.

"We f...

## Damage is rivaled by shock

Near the epicenter, Los Gatos suffers ruined homes, shops

By W. JOSEPH CAMPBELL
*Courant Staff Writer*

LOS GATOS, Calif. — By the acre Wednesday, the curious and the sympathetic approached the awesome wreckage of a century-old Victorian mansion, a survivor of the great earthquake of 1906 but a victim in the northern California temblor Tuesday.

Sometimes they would ask the owner, Lynbet Wright, whether she minded. "If you can stand tragedy, go ahead. Be my guest," she replied, to bitterness in her voice.

The huge and included house, Wright said was built by a ...

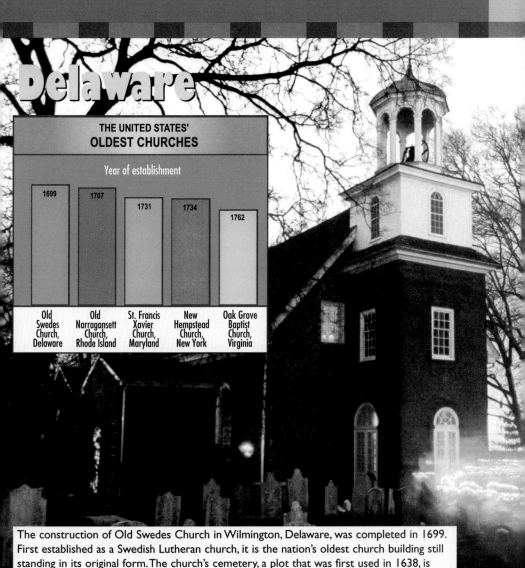

## Delaware

**THE UNITED STATES'
OLDEST CHURCHES**

Year of establishment

| Old Swedes Church, Delaware | Old Narragansett Church, Rhode Island | St. Francis Xavier Church, Maryland | New Hempstead Church, New York | Oak Grove Baptist Church, Virginia |
|---|---|---|---|---|
| 1699 | 1707 | 1731 | 1734 | 1762 |

The construction of Old Swedes Church in Wilmington, Delaware, was completed in 1699. First established as a Swedish Lutheran church, it is the nation's oldest church building still standing in its original form. The church's cemetery, a plot that was first used in 1638, is believed to hold many of Delaware's first settlers. In fact, when the church was constructed near the cemetery, the foundation was built around a number of early plots giving it an unusual shape. Old Swedes Church was designated a National Historic Landmark in 1963.

# State with the
# Warmest City

## Florida

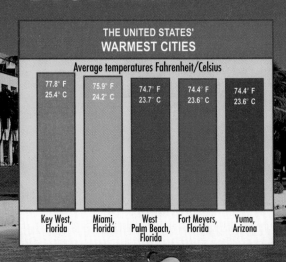

**THE UNITED STATES' WARMEST CITIES**

Average temperatures Fahrenheit/Celsius

| Key West, Florida | Miami, Florida | West Palm Beach, Florida | Fort Meyers, Florida | Yuma, Arizona |
|---|---|---|---|---|
| 77.8° F 25.4° C | 75.9° F 24.2° C | 74.7° F 23.7° C | 74.4° F 23.6° C | 74.4° F 23.6° C |

Temperatures in Key West, Florida, maintain a yearly average of 77.8° Fahrenheit (25.4° C). Even winter temperatures rarely get below 40° Fahrenheit (4.4° C). In fact, none of the Florida Keys have ever had frost. Key West—also the southernmost city within the United States—is about 100 miles (161 km) south of the Florida mainland. To reach the island, drivers must use the Overseas Highway. It is made up of a series of 42 bridges and is the longest overwater road in the world. The longest bridge in the Keys has a span of 7 miles (11 km).

# State That Produces the Most Peanuts

## Georgia

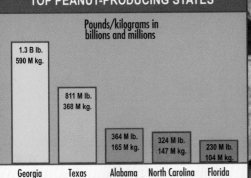

THE UNITED STATES'
**TOP PEANUT-PRODUCING STATES**

Pounds/kilograms in billions and millions

| Georgia | Texas | Alabama | North Carolina | Florida |
|---|---|---|---|---|
| 1.3 B lb. 590 M kg. | 811 M lb. 368 M kg. | 364 M lb. 165 M kg. | 324 M lb. 147 M kg. | 230 M lb. 104 M kg. |

Each year, Georgia harvests approximately 520,000 acres (210,441 ha) of peanut plants on 4,700 farms. This produces a crop of nuts weighing more than 1.3 billion pounds (590 million kg)! That's almost 50% of the nation's total peanut production. Georgia's crop also makes up about one-half of the nuts used to make peanut butter. About 60% of the peanuts exported overseas are from Georgia, generating about $150 million for the United States.

# State with the World's
# Wettest Place

Hawaii

Mount Waialeale, located on the island of Kauai, receives about 460 inches (1,168 cm) of rain each year! Waialeale is located on Alakai Swamp—a plateau on the side of an extinct volcanic depression. It is 5,148 feet (1,569 m) high and is often surrounded by rain clouds. In 1982, Waialeale received 666 inches (1,692 cm) of rain and set an all-time world record. In contrast, the city of Kawaihae, located on the island of Hawaii, receives only about 9 inches (23 cm) of rain each year.

### THE UNITED STATES'
### WETTEST PLACES

Annual rainfall in inches/centimeters

| Mt. Waialeale, Hawaii | Mobile, Alabama | New Orleans, Louisiana | Miami, Florida | Charleston, South Carolina |
|---|---|---|---|---|
| 460 in. 1,168 cm. | 86 in. 218 cm. | 79 in. 201 cm. | 70 in. 178 cm. | 67 in. 170 cm. |

# State with the Largest Raptor Habitat

## Idaho

The Snake River Birds of Prey National Conservation Area is located along 81 miles (130 km) of the Snake River in Idaho. This rugged land is home to approximately 2,500 nesting raptors, or birds of prey. The birds stay there from mid-March until late June. Nesting raptor species found here include golden eagles, red-tailed hawks, barn owls, and turkey vultures. Many of the birds, including the 200 pairs of prairie falcons, are drawn to the area because of its abundant prey.

### THE UNITED STATES' LARGEST RAPTOR HABITATS

Average number of birds during peak times

| Location | Birds |
| --- | --- |
| Snake River, Idaho | 2,500 |
| Chilkat River, Alaska | 2,400 |
| Bear Valley, Oregon | 1,000 |
| Lake Taneycomo, Missouri | 700 |
| Skagit River, Washington | 350 |

119

# State with the
# Tallest Building

## Illinois

The Sears Tower, located in Chicago, rises 1,450 feet (442 m) above the ground. That's one-quarter of a mile high. If you include the spires, the total height of the building grows to 1,707 feet (520 m). The Sears Tower is the world's second-tallest inhabitable building. It has 110 floors and 4.5 million square feet (.4 million sq m) of office space. If this floor space was laid out on one level, it would cover 16 city blocks. The Sears Tower weighs more than 222,500 tons (201,852 t) and cost $160 million to build.

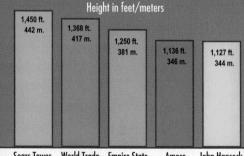

### THE UNITED STATES' TALLEST BUILDINGS

Height in feet/meters

| Sears Tower, Illinois | World Trade Center, NY 1970-2001 | Empire State Building, New York | Amoco Building, Illinois | John Hancock Center, Illinois |
|---|---|---|---|---|
| 1,450 ft. 442 m. | 1,368 ft. 417 m. | 1,250 ft. 381 m. | 1,136 ft. 346 m. | 1,127 ft. 344 m. |

# State with the Largest Children's Museum

## Indiana

### THE UNITED STATES' LARGEST CHILDREN'S MUSEUMS

Size in square feet/ square meters

| Children's Museum of Indianapolis, Indiana | Chicago Children's Museum, Illinios | The Children's Museum, Washington | Garden State Discovery Museum, New Jersey | Boston Children's Museum, Massachusetts |
|---|---|---|---|---|
| 356,000 sq. ft. 33,072 sq. m. | 57,000 sq. ft. 5,295 sq. m. | 32,200 sq. ft. 2,991 sq. m. | 20,000 sq. ft. 1,858 sq. m. | 10,000 sq. ft. 929 sq. m. |

The Children's Museum of Indianapolis is a giant, 356,000-square-foot (33,072.4-sq-m) facility on 13 acres (5.3 ha) that houses 10 major galleries. Every year, families from all corners of the United States and Canada—approximately 1 million people—come to experience the wide variety of kid-friendly exhibits. Some permanent exhibits include SpaceQuest Planetarium, Passport to the World, Indianapolis 500 Mile Race Car, and Mysteries in History. The 310-seat CineDome theater features a 76-foot- (23-m) high domed screen.

121

# State That Produces the Most Corn

## Iowa

Iowa grows about 1.65 billion bushels (.58 billion hl) of corn each year! That's enough to give each person in the United States about 6 bushels (2.1 hl) of corn. Most of this state's corn, however, is raised for livestock feed. Iowa's corn-fed cattle and hogs are another large source of Iowa's income. Some of Iowa's corn is sold to make food products— the state is a major producer of popcorn. Level land and rich soil provide Iowa with the perfect farming environment. In fact, the state produces 10% of the nation's total food supply.

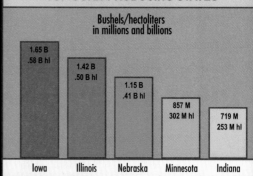

**THE UNITED STATES'
TOP CORN-PRODUCING STATES**

Bushels/hectoliters
in millions and billions

| Iowa | Illinois | Nebraska | Minnesota | Indiana |
|------|----------|----------|-----------|---------|
| 1.65 B .58 B hl | 1.42 B .50 B hl | 1.15 B .41 B hl | 857 M 302 M hl | 719 M 253 M hl |

# State with the Largest
# Ball of Twine

## Kansas

A giant ball of twine that resides in Cawker City, Kansas, weighs more than 17,000 pounds (7,711 kg) and has a 40-foot (12-m) circumference. The ball is 11 feet (3.4 m) tall and is made up of 1,140 miles (1,835 km) of twine. Frank Stoeber created the ball on his farm in 1953 from twine that he used to wrap hay bales. Cawker City assumed ownership of the twine ball in 1961, and holds a twine-a-thon each year in conjunction with the annual picnic. In 1998, about 33,000 feet (10,058 m) of twine was added by the town's 800 residents.

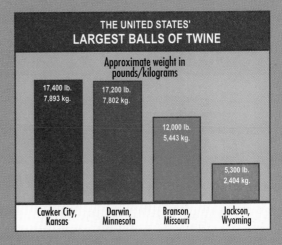

### THE UNITED STATES' LARGEST BALLS OF TWINE

Approximate weight in pounds/kilograms

| Cawker City, Kansas | Darwin, Minnesota | Branson, Missouri | Jackson, Wyoming |
|---|---|---|---|
| 17,400 lb. 7,893 kg. | 17,200 lb. 7,802 kg. | 12,000 lb. 5,443 kg. | 5,300 lb. 2,404 kg. |

# State with the World's
# Longest Cave System

## Kentucky

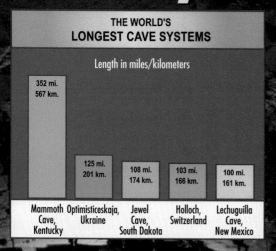

**THE WORLD'S LONGEST CAVE SYSTEMS**

Length in miles/kilometers

| Cave | Length |
|------|--------|
| Mammoth Cave, Kentucky | 352 mi. / 567 km. |
| Optimisticeskaja, Ukraine | 125 mi. / 201 km. |
| Jewel Cave, South Dakota | 108 mi. / 174 km. |
| Holloch, Switzerland | 103 mi. / 166 km. |
| Lechuguilla Cave, New Mexico | 100 mi. / 161 km. |

Kentucky's Mammoth Cave is a complex system of tunnels that extends for more than 350 miles (563 km). Some scientists believe there are still sections of the cave yet to be discovered. This giant underground world has fascinated visitors since prehistoric times. In fact, many ancient artifacts and tools have been located there. Today, about 500,000 people visit the cave each year. They marvel at the stalagmite formations, bottomless pits, and underground rooms. Animals are also drawn to Mammoth Cave. About 130 different species can be found there, including bats, salamanders, and many types of insects.

# State with the Largest Indoor Arena

Louisiana's world-famous Superdome is the official home of pro football's New Orleans Saints. When it is filled to capacity, the arena can hold up to 95,000 fans and spectators. The structure covers a total of 13 acres (5.3 ha) and has 125 million cubic feet (3.54 million cubic m) of interior space. The giant dome is 680 feet (207 m) in diameter and is supported by 96 columns. The Superdome was completed in 1975 at a cost of $163 million. Since then, it has hosted gymnastics events, professional baseball and basketball competitions, and several Super Bowls.

**THE UNITED STATES' LARGEST INDOOR ARENAS**

Maximum seating capacity

| Louisiana Superdome, Louisiana | Georgia Dome, Georgia | Cotton Dome, Texas | RCA Dome, Indiana | Enron Field, Texas |
|---|---|---|---|---|
| 95,000 | 80,000 | 68,252 | 61,639 | 40,950 |

## Louisiana

# State That Harvests the Most Lobsters

Maine's fishers harvested more than 47 million pounds (21.3 million kg) of lobsters, which generated about $137.2 million in revenues in 1998. That's enough to feed the entire population of California and Florida a lobster dinner. American lobsters are found off the Atlantic coast from Canada to North Carolina. Although they are considered a delicacy today, early Americans disliked lobster and used them as garden fertilizer. In fact, prisoners were often made to eat lobster several times a week.

## THE STATES THAT HARVEST THE MOST LOBSTERS

Lobsters harvested in millions of pounds/kilograms

|  |  |
|-------|--------|
| Maine | 47 M lb. / 21.3 M kg. |
| Massachusetts | 13.2 M lb. / 6 M kg. |
| New York | 8.5 M lb. / 3.8 M kg. |
| Connecticut | 3.5 M lb. / 1.6 M kg. |

## Maine

# State with the Oldest
# Music School

# Maryland

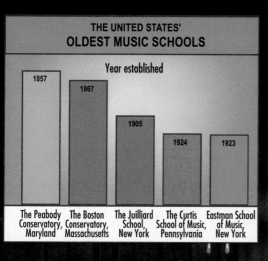

**THE UNITED STATES'
OLDEST MUSIC SCHOOLS**

Year established

| The Peabody Conservatory, Maryland | The Boston Conservatory, Massachusetts | The Juilliard School, New York | The Curtis School of Music, Pennsylvania | Eastman School of Music, New York |
|---|---|---|---|---|
| 1857 | 1867 | 1905 | 1924 | 1923 |

The Peabody Conservatory of Music was founded in Maryland in 1857. The actual opening of the school was delayed for nearly 9 years however—until 1866 because of the Civil War. There are approximately 600 pupils enrolled in the school today, and about one-third of them are international students. The Peabody Conservatory offers degree programs in many different fields, including jazz, music theater, and music management. The school also offers concerts to the public on a regular basis.

# State with the Oldest
# Lighthouse Site

## Massachusetts

Boston Light first lit up the harbor in September of 1716, making it the first lighthouse used in North America. Located on Little Brewster Island, the original lighthouse tower was destroyed by the British during the American Revolution. A new tower was built in 1783. Today, Boston Light is the only lighthouse in the United States that is operated by a person, instead of being automated. This National Historic Landmark is 89 feet (27 m) tall and made of stone. Its white light flashes every 10 seconds.

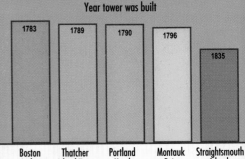

**THE UNITED STATES'**
**OLDEST LIGHTHOUSES**

Year tower was built

| Boston Light, Massachusetts | Thatcher Island Twin Lighthouses, Massachusetts | Portland Head Light, Maine | Montauk Point Lighthouse, New York | Straightsmouth Island Lighthouse, Massachusetts |
|---|---|---|---|---|
| 1783 | 1789 | 1790 | 1796 | 1835 |

# State with the Snowiest City

## Michigan

The city of Marquette, which is located in the northern part of Michigan, receives an average of 130 inches (330 cm) of snow each year. That's enough snow to easily bury a school bus. The main reason for Marquette's severe weather is its location. Michigan's Upper Peninsula lies between Lake Superior and Lake Michigan. The moist winds that swirl off these lakes create cold weather and heavy snowstorms. Even in the summer, the area has an average temperature of only 65° Fahrenheit (18° C).

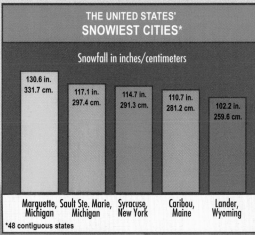

**THE UNITED STATES'
SNOWIEST CITIES***

Snowfall in inches/centimeters

| City | Snowfall |
|------|----------|
| Marquette, Michigan | 130.6 in. / 331.7 cm. |
| Sault Ste. Marie, Michigan | 117.1 in. / 297.4 cm. |
| Syracuse, New York | 114.7 in. / 291.3 cm. |
| Caribou, Maine | 110.7 in. / 281.2 cm. |
| Lander, Wyoming | 102.2 in. / 259.6 cm. |

*48 contiguous states

129

# State with the Coldest City

## Minnesota

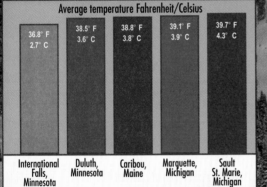

**THE UNITED STATES' COLDEST CITIES**

Average temperature Fahrenheit/Celsius

| International Falls, Minnesota | Duluth, Minnesota | Caribou, Maine | Marquette, Michigan | Sault St. Marie, Michigan |
|---|---|---|---|---|
| 36.8° F 2.7° C | 38.5° F 3.6° C | 38.8° F 3.8° C | 39.1° F 3.9° C | 39.7° F 4.3° C |

International Falls, Minnesota, has an average temperature of 36.8°Fahrenheit (2.67°C) year-round. During the winter, temperatures often stay well below freezing. The city is located in the northern tip of the state, on the border of the subarctic forest in Ontario, Canada. International Falls will sometimes even get frost during the summer months. During the winter, the annual snowfall may reach up to 70 inches (178 cm).

# State with the Largest
# Blues Music Collection

# Mississippi

## THE UNITED STATES' LARGEST BLUES COLLECTIONS

Number of recordings held

| University of Mississippi, Mississippi | National Ragtime and Jazz Archive, Illinois | Jazz Society of Oregon, Oregon | Chicago Blues Archive, Illinois |
|---|---|---|---|
| 50,000 | 20,000 | 6,000 | 3,000 |

The University of Mississippi's Blues Archive has approximately 50,000 blues recordings in the form of records, albums, compact discs, and videos. What began as a hobby for librarian John Sikes Hartin in 1966 has turned into the largest collection of blues recordings in the world. Some recordings include B.B. King, Mamie Smith, Sonny Boy Williamson, and Charlie Parker. In addition to recordings, the Blues Archive also has many books, posters, autographs, and written correspondence by famous blues musicians.

# State with the Tallest Human-Made Monument

## Missouri

The Gateway Arch in St. Louis towers 630 feet (192 m) above the ground. It is tall enough to be seen from up to 30 miles (48 km) away! Built in 1965, this monument was first known as the Jefferson National Expansion Memorial. It was built to remind the world that St. Louis played an important part in the westward expansion of the United States. A tram inside the arch carries people to an observation area at the top. On a busy day, some 5,500 people ride the arch's tram and get a spectacular view of the city.

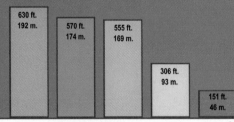

### THE UNITED STATES' TALLEST HUMAN-MADE MONUMENTS

Height in feet/meters

| Gateway Arch, Missouri | San Jacinto Monument, Texas | Washington Monument, Washington DC | Bennington Monument, Vermont | Statue of Liberty, New York |
|---|---|---|---|---|
| 630 ft. 192 m. | 570 ft. 174 m. | 555 ft. 169 m. | 306 ft. 93 m. | 151 ft. 46 m. |

# State with the Oldest National Monument

## Montana

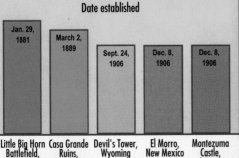

### THE UNITED STATES' OLDEST NATIONAL MONUMENTS

**Date established**

| Little Big Horn Battlefield, Montana | Casa Grande Ruins, Arizona | Devil's Tower, Wyoming | El Morro, New Mexico | Montezuma Castle, Arizona |
|---|---|---|---|---|
| Jan. 29, 1881 | March 2, 1889 | Sept. 24, 1906 | Dec. 8, 1906 | Dec. 8, 1906 |

The Little Big Horn Battlefield National Monument, located near Crow Agency, Montana, was first designated a national cemetery in 1879. A memorial was built on Last Stand Hill two years later to commemorate the Seventh Cavalry soldiers who died there. Today, the complex also has a museum, hiking trails, and a research library. The Battle of Little Big Horn took place on June 25 and 26, 1876. General George Custer and the Seventh Calvary were defeated by the Lakota, Cheyenne, and Arapaho.

# State with the Most
# Sandhill Cranes

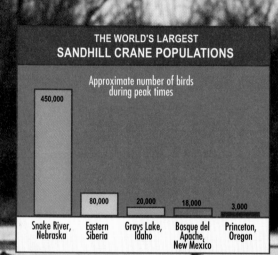

THE WORLD'S LARGEST
SANDHILL CRANE POPULATIONS

Approximate number of birds
during peak times

| Snake River, Nebraska | Eastern Siberia | Grays Lake, Idaho | Bosque del Apache, New Mexico | Princeton, Oregon |
|---|---|---|---|---|
| 450,000 | 80,000 | 20,000 | 18,000 | 3,000 |

For approximately five weeks each spring, Nebraska is the resting spot for 400,000 to 500,000 sandhill cranes. That's about 75% of the world's sandhill crane population! As part of their annual migration, these birds arrive from Texas, New Mexico, California, and Arizona to feed and rest along a 150-mile (241-km) stretch of the Platte River between Grand Isle and Sutherland. The residents of this area celebrate the cranes' arrival—along with the arrival of 10 million ducks and geese—during the Spring Wing Ding celebration in Clay Center.

Nebraska

# State with the Driest Climate

## Nevada

The driest area of Nevada is located in the state's southeastern region. The average rainfall there rarely exceeds 4 inches (10 cm) per year! Even in the northwest mountains, the annual rainfall only averages 23 inches (58 cm). One reason for Nevada's lack of rain is the Sierra-Nevada Mountain range that borders the state to the west. Its high peaks often cause clouds that come from the Pacific to drop their rain before they can reach Nevada. Despite the dry climate, many plants thrive here. Yucca, cacti, mesquite, creosote, Joshua trees, and sagebrush are all abundant.

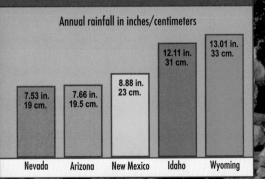

### THE UNITED STATES' DRIEST CLIMATES

Annual rainfall in inches/centimeters

| Nevada | Arizona | New Mexico | Idaho | Wyoming |
|--------|---------|------------|-------|---------|
| 7.53 in. 19 cm. | 7.66 in. 19.5 cm. | 8.88 in. 23 cm. | 12.11 in. 31 cm. | 13.01 in. 33 cm. |

# State with the Oldest
# Covered Bridge

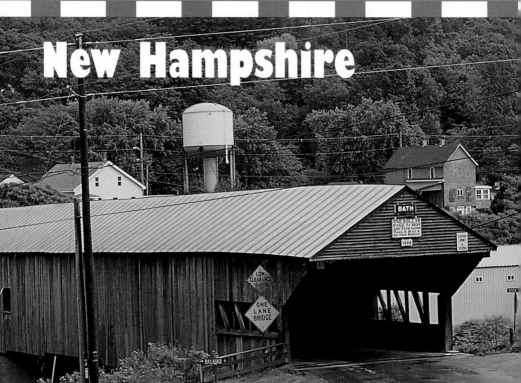

## New Hampshire

The Haverhill-Bath Covered Bridge in New Hampshire was completed in 1832. It has a two-lane span of 278 feet (85 m) and crosses the Ammonoosuc River to connect the towns of Haverhill and Bath. Until 1999, the bridge had been open to cars and trucks. But because of its narrow width and the high cost of renovating the bridge, it is now only open to pedestrians and bicyclists. Today, New Hampshire has approximately 55 remaining covered bridges, but the number is shrinking due to deterioration from cold, harsh weather, vandalism, and neglect.

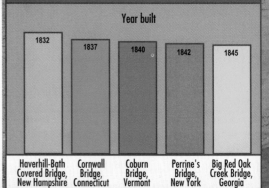

THE UNITED STATES'
**OLDEST COVERED BRIDGES**

Year built

| 1832 | 1837 | 1840 | 1842 | 1845 |
|------|------|------|------|------|
| Haverhill-Bath Covered Bridge, New Hampshire | Cornwall Bridge, Connecticut | Coburn Bridge, Vermont | Perrine's Bridge, New York | Big Red Oak Creek Bridge, Georgia |

# State That Is Most Densely Populated

## New Jersey

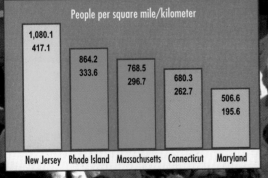

### THE STATES WITH THE HIGHEST POPULATION DENSITY

People per square mile/kilometer

| New Jersey | Rhode Island | Massachusetts | Connecticut | Maryland |
|---|---|---|---|---|
| 1,080.1 | 864.2 | 768.5 | 680.3 | 506.6 |
| 417.1 | 333.6 | 296.7 | 262.7 | 195.6 |

The population of the tiny state of New Jersey averages 1,080 people per square mile (417 per sq km). Even though it is the fifth smallest state in area, it is the ninth most populated. By comparison, New Jersey would fit inside the state of Alaska 73 times, but New Jersey's population is 14 times larger! New Jersey has a high population because it is near New York City and Philadelphia, where many New Jersey residents work. Thanks to its many commuters, New Jersey's transportation system is one of the largest and busiest in the world.

137

# State with the World's Largest Balloon Festival

## New Mexico

Each October, approximately 1,000 hot air and gas-filled balloons take part in the Kodak Albuquerque International Balloon Fiesta in the skies over New Mexico. This event draws balloons from around the world, and is often seen in more than 50 countries. The festival takes place in the 350-acre (142-ha) Balloon Fiesta State Park. In addition to the balloon races, flights, and exhibits, the event also features musicians, fireworks, street entertainers, and a broad selection of New Mexican food.

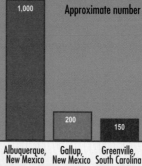

THE WORLD'S
**LARGEST BALLOON FESTIVALS**

Approximate number of balloons

| | |
|---|---|
| 1,000 | Albuquerque, New Mexico |
| 200 | Gallup, New Mexico |
| 150 | Greenville, South Carolina |
| 150 | Gatineau, Canada |
| 125 | Reno, Nevada |

# State with the
# Longest Bridge

## New York

The Verrazano-Narrows Bridge has a main span of 4,260 feet (1,298 m) and connects Brooklyn to Staten Island. The roadway alone weighs 60,000 tons (54, 432 t) and is suspended about 230 feet (70 m) above New York Harbor. It is supported by four large cables that are secured to 690-foot- (210-m) high towers. Each cable weighs an incredible 10,000 tons (9,072 t). The main span has two levels, each with two six-lane roads. The bridge was completed in 1964 at a cost of $325 million. It held the record for the world's longest bridge until the Humber Bridge in England was built in 1981.

### THE UNITED STATES' LONGEST BRIDGES

Length of main span in feet/meters

| Verrazano-Narrows, New York | Golden Gate, California | Mackinaw Straits, Michigan | George Washington, New York | Tacoma Narrows, Washington |
|---|---|---|---|---|
| 4,260 ft. 1,298 m. | 4,200 ft. 1,280 m. | 3,800 ft. 1,158 m. | 3,500 ft. 1,067 m. | 2,800 ft. 853 m. |

# State with the Oldest
# State University

## North Carolina

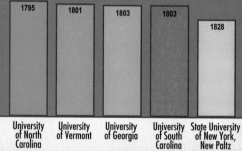

### THE UNITED STATES'
### OLDEST PUBLIC UNIVERSITIES

Year established

| University of North Carolina | University of Vermont | University of Georgia | University of South Carolina | State University of New York, New Paltz |
|---|---|---|---|---|
| 1795 | 1801 | 1803 | 1803 | 1828 |

The University of North Carolina was founded in 1789 but did not accept its first student until February of 1795 because of a lack of funding. By the following month, the university consisted of 2 buildings, 2 professors, and 41 students. Today, the University of North Carolina has more than 15,000 undergraduates and 2,400 faculty. It is continually ranked by *U.S. News and World Report* as one of the top 30 universities in the nation. Some famous UNC graduates include President James Polk, actor Andy Griffith, and sports superstars Michael Jordan and Mia Hamm.

# State with the Largest
# Hoofed Mammal

# North Dakota

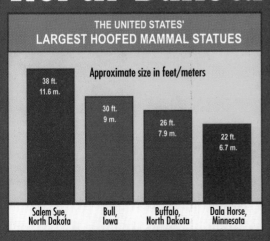

THE UNITED STATES'
## LARGEST HOOFED MAMMAL STATUES

Approximate size in feet/meters

| | | | |
|---|---|---|---|
| 38 ft. 11.6 m. | 30 ft. 9 m. | 26 ft. 7.9 m. | 22 ft. 6.7 m. |
| Salem Sue, North Dakota | Bull, Iowa | Buffalo, North Dakota | Dala Horse, Minnesota |

"Salem Sue" is truly a large cow. She stands 38 feet (11.6 m) above the fields that surround her and weighs about 12,000 pounds (5,443 kg). Salem Sue measures 50 feet (15m) long and is made out of fiberglass. The world's largest Holstein was built in 1974 and cost approximately $40,000. She was funded by area farmers, businesspeople, and local residents to celebrate New Salem's success in the dairy industry. The New Salem Lions organized the initial project and today continue to keep up Salem Sue's maintenance. Salem Sue also has a regional friend— North Dakota has the world's largest buffalo statue.

# State with the Largest Twins Gathering

## Ohio

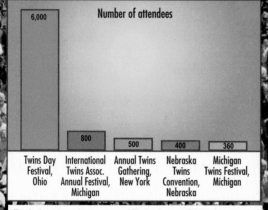

THE STATES WITH THE LARGEST TWINS GATHERINGS

Number of attendees

| | Number of attendees |
|---|---|
| 6,000 | Twins Day Festival, Ohio |
| 800 | International Twins Assoc. Annual Festival, Michigan |
| 500 | Annual Twins Gathering, New York |
| 400 | Nebraska Twins Convention, Nebraska |
| 360 | Michigan Twins Festival, Michigan |

Each August, the town of Twinsburg, Ohio, hosts about 6,000 twins at its annual Twins Day Festival. Both identical and fraternal twins from around the world participate, and many dress alike. The twins take part in games, parades, and contests, such as the oldest identical twins and the twins with the widest combined smile. The event began in 1976, in honor of Aaron and Moses Wilcox, twin brothers who inspired the city to adopt its name in 1817. The festival began as a gathering of local twins, and developed into one of the largest twins festivals in the world.

# State with the Largest Military Museum

# Oklahoma

The 45th Infantry Division Museum, located in Oklahoma City, Oklahoma, is spread over 12.5 acres (5 ha). Its seven galleries display thousands of exhibits and artifacts related to the military history of Oklahoma. Some displays include exhibits that date back to 1541. Other galleries feature artifacts that take visitors through World War II and Desert Storm. The museum also features 200 of Bill Mauldin's original "Willie and Joe" cartoons about two riflemen in World War II, Korean-era artillery, original uniforms, and dioramas. The outdoor Military Park has more than 50 military vehicles, aircraft, and artillery.

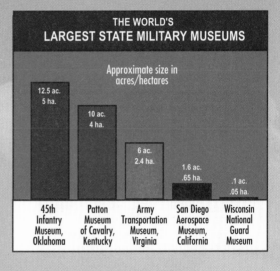

**THE WORLD'S LARGEST STATE MILITARY MUSEUMS**

Approximate size in acres/hectares

| 45th Infantry Museum, Oklahoma | Patton Museum of Cavalry, Kentucky | Army Transportation Museum, Virginia | San Diego Aerospace Museum, California | Wisconsin National Guard Museum |
|---|---|---|---|---|
| 12.5 ac. 5 ha. | 10 ac. 4 ha. | 6 ac. 2.4 ha. | 1.6 ac. .65 ha. | .1 ac. .05 ha. |

# State with the World's
# Longest Sea Cave

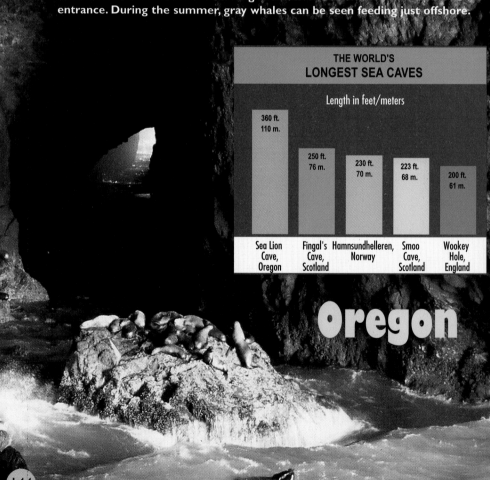

Sea Lion Cave, located on the Pacific coast of Oregon, reaches a length of 360 feet (110 m). That's the same length as a football field. The cave is also 120 feet (37 m) from floor to ceiling. Sea Lion Cave began to form approximately 25 million years ago. One of the most amazing things about this natural wonder is its inhabitants. Many sea lions live here year-round, spending their winters in the cave and their summers sunning themselves out on the rocks at the cave's entrance. During the summer, gray whales can be seen feeding just offshore.

## THE WORLD'S LONGEST SEA CAVES

Length in feet/meters

| Sea Lion Cave, Oregon | Fingal's Cave, Scotland | Hamnsundhelleren, Norway | Smoo Cave, Scotland | Wookey Hole, England |
|---|---|---|---|---|
| 360 ft. 110 m. | 250 ft. 76 m. | 230 ft. 70 m. | 223 ft. 68 m. | 200 ft. 61 m. |

## Oregon

# State with the Largest Candy Producer

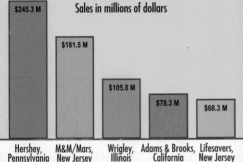

**THE UNITED STATES' LARGEST CANDY PRODUCERS**

Sales in millions of dollars

- $245.3 M — Hershey, Pennsylvania
- $181.5 M — M&M/Mars, New Jersey
- $105.8 M — Wrigley, Illinois
- $78.3 M — Adams & Brooks, California
- $68.3 M — Lifesavers, New Jersey

Hershey Chocolate North America is the United States' leading domestic producer of chocolate and non-chocolate candy, with annual sales of more than $245 million. The candy-producing facilities, located in the town named after Milton Hershey and his empire, are capable of making 33 million Hershey's Kisses each day. Some other best-selling Hershey's products include Almond Joy, Mounds, Kit Kat, Reese's Peanut Butter Cups, Jolly Ranchers, and Twizzlers. Hershey exports its candy to more than 90 countries worldwide.

# Pennsylvania

# State with the Smallest Area

# Rhode Island

Rhode Island covers just 1,545 square miles (4,002 sq km). In fact, the longest distance from north to south measures just 48 miles (77 km). Rhode Island is, however, a very densely populated state. Nearly 1 million people live in its five counties. That means there are about 947 people for each square mile of land. Providence is the state's largest city with a population of just over 150,000. Many tourists are also drawn to Rhode Island for summer recreation. With its 400 miles (644 km) of coastline, the state is a popular beach destination.

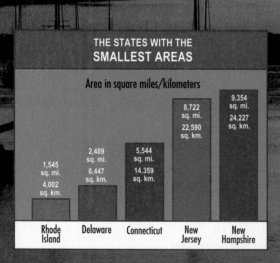

THE STATES WITH THE
SMALLEST AREAS

Area in square miles/kilometers

| | | | | |
|---|---|---|---|---|
| 1,545 sq. mi. 4,002 sq. km. | 2,489 sq. mi. 6,447 sq. km. | 5,544 sq. mi. 14,359 sq. km. | 8,722 sq. mi. 22,590 sq. km. | 9,354 sq. mi. 24,227 sq. km. |
| Rhode Island | Delaware | Connecticut | New Jersey | New Hampshire |

# State with the
# Oldest Museum

## South Carolina

**THE UNITED STATES'
OLDEST MUSEUMS**

Year founded

| | | | | |
|---|---|---|---|---|
| 1773 | 1799 | 1809 | 1824 | 1866 |
| Charleston Museum, South Carolina | Peabody Essex Museum, Massachusetts | NY Historical Society Museum, New York | Pilgrim Hall Museum, Massachusetts | Peabody Museum of Archaeology, Massachusetts |

The Charleston Museum, located in Charleston, South Carolina, was founded in 1773. The museum's displays and collections tell the social and natural history of one of America's most important port towns and coastal regions. Some exhibits focus on early Native Americans, the plantation system, the Civil War, and African-American history. Artifacts and displays at the Charleston Museum include clothing, toys, photographs, furniture, and games. The museum also runs the Second Saturday program—a monthly family day with a fun, educational focus.

# State with the Largest
# Portrait Bust

## South Dakota

Mount Rushmore National Memorial, located in the Black Hills of South Dakota, features a 500-foot- (152-m) high portrait bust of four American presidents. The faces of George Washington, Thomas Jefferson, Abraham Lincoln, and Theodore Roosevelt are each about 60 feet (18.3 m) high. Gutzon Borglum began to carve this monument in 1927, but the work took 14 years to complete. The entire project cost only about $1 million. More than 2 million people visit the memorial each year.

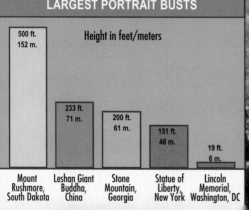

THE WORLD'S
LARGEST PORTRAIT BUSTS

Height in feet/meters

| | | | | |
|---|---|---|---|---|
| 500 ft. 152 m. | 233 ft. 71 m. | 200 ft. 61 m. | 151 ft. 46 m. | 19 ft. 6 m. |
| Mount Rushmore, South Dakota | Leshan Giant Buddha, China | Stone Mountain, Georgia | Statue of Liberty, New York | Lincoln Memorial, Washington, DC |

# State with the Most-Winning Women's NCAA Team

## Tennessee

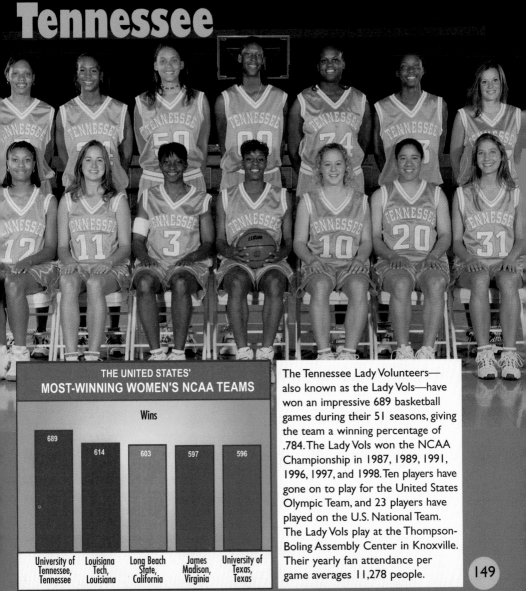

### THE UNITED STATES' MOST-WINNING WOMEN'S NCAA TEAMS

**Wins**

| University of Tennessee, Tennessee | Louisiana Tech, Louisiana | Long Beach State, California | James Madison, Virginia | University of Texas, Texas |
|---|---|---|---|---|
| 689 | 614 | 603 | 597 | 596 |

The Tennessee Lady Volunteers—also known as the Lady Vols—have won an impressive 689 basketball games during their 51 seasons, giving the team a winning percentage of .784. The Lady Vols won the NCAA Championship in 1987, 1989, 1991, 1996, 1997, and 1998. Ten players have gone on to play for the United States Olympic Team, and 23 players have played on the U.S. National Team. The Lady Vols play at the Thompson-Boling Assembly Center in Knoxville. Their yearly fan attendance per game averages 11,278 people.

149

# State with the
# Most Farmland

## Texas

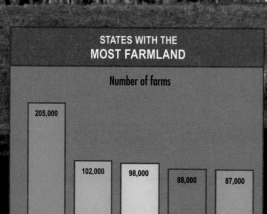

### STATES WITH THE MOST FARMLAND

#### Number of farms

| | | | | |
|---|---|---|---|---|
| 205,000 | 102,000 | 98,000 | 88,000 | 87,000 |
| Texas | Missouri | Iowa | Kentucky | Minnesota |

With more than 200,000 farms and 129 million acres (5.2 million ha) of farmland, Texas is one of the top producers of many U.S. crops. It continually leads the nation in cotton and cottonseed production. Texas is also the nation's second-largest producer of watermelons and honeydew melons. Other important crops include pecans, peanuts, oats, barley, and corn. Parts of eastern Texas are known for their huge rice crops. Texas also raises more beef cattle and sheep than any other state.

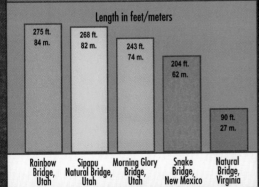

# State with the Largest
# Natural Stone Bridge

# Utah

## THE UNITED STATES'
## LARGEST NATURAL STONE BRIDGES

Length in feet/meters

| Bridge | Length |
|---|---|
| Rainbow Bridge, Utah | 275 ft. / 84 m. |
| Sipapu Natural Bridge, Utah | 268 ft. / 82 m. |
| Morning Glory Bridge, Utah | 243 ft. / 74 m. |
| Snake Bridge, New Mexico | 204 ft. / 62 m. |
| Natural Bridge, Virginia | 90 ft. / 27 m. |

The Rainbow Bridge National Monument near Lake Powell in Utah has a span of 275 feet (84 m). This incredible natural stone arch reaches a height of 290 feet (88 m) and is 33 feet (10 m) wide. The midsection of Rainbow Bridge is about 42 feet (13 m) thick. The bridge is made up of multi-colored sandstones, iron oxide, and magnesium—substances that have a colorful glow in sunlight. Many Native Americans, including the Navajo, whose land surrounds the arch, consider Rainbow Bridge a sacred place because rainbows are considered guardians of the universe.

# State with the World's Oldest Coral Reef

## Vermont

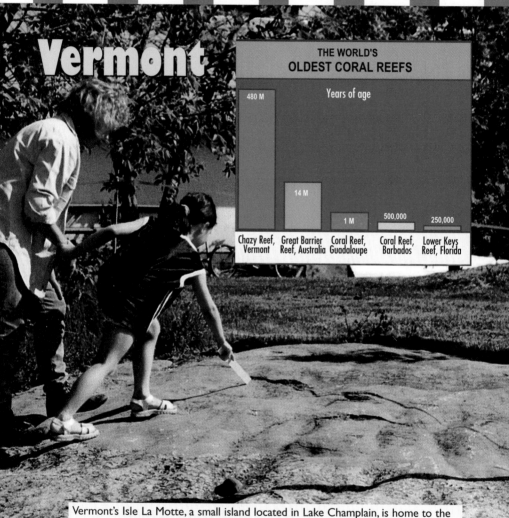

**THE WORLD'S OLDEST CORAL REEFS**

Years of age

| Chazy Reef, Vermont | Great Barrier Reef, Australia | Coral Reef, Guadaloupe | Coral Reef, Barbados | Lower Keys Reef, Florida |
|---|---|---|---|---|
| 480 M | 14 M | 1 M | 500,000 | 250,000 |

Vermont's Isle La Motte, a small island located in Lake Champlain, is home to the remnants of a coral reef that dates back more than 480 million years. That means the Chazy Reef formed before dinosaurs roamed the earth. The reef is now visible on dry land, but it actually formed in a shallow sea when the North American continent was still near the equator. Part of the reef is located in Fisk Quarry, and it has been preserved for scientific research. Today, the unique features and unequaled age of the Chazy Reef helps scientists answer questions about the history and formation of the earth and seas.

# Birthplace of the Most Presidents

## Virginia

The Commonwealth of Virginia has earned the nickname "the Mother of Presidents" because eight of America's chief executives were born there. These presidents are George Washington (1st; 1789–1797), Thomas Jefferson (3rd; 1801–1809), James Madison (4th; 1809–1817), James Monroe (5th; 1817–1825), William Henry Harrison (9th; 1841), John Tyler (10th; 1841–1845), Zachary Taylor (12th; 1849–1850), and Woodrow Wilson (28th; 1913–1921). Today, two of Virginia's top tourist attractions are Mt. Vernon and Monticello, the birthplaces of Washington and Jefferson.

### BIRTHPLACES OF THE MOST PRESIDENTS

Presidents born in the state

| Virginia | Ohio | Massachusetts | New York | Texas |
|----------|------|---------------|----------|-------|
| 8 | 7 | 4 | 4 | 3 |

Monticello

153

# State That Produces the Most Apples

In just one year, the state of Washington produces an average of about 4.9 billion pounds (2.2 billion kg) of apples. That's enough to give every person in the world 18 pounds (8 kg) of apples a year. The Columbia Basin, located in the central part of Washington, is where most of the state's produce is grown. Its fertile, well-drained soil is ideal for apple trees. In the United States, about one-half of the annual apple crop is sold as fresh fruit. Another one-fifth of the apple crop is used for juice, jelly, apple butter, and vinegar.

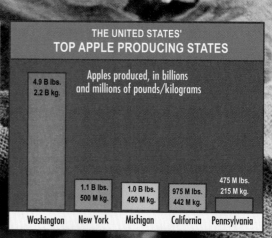

**THE UNITED STATES' TOP APPLE PRODUCING STATES**

Apples produced, in billions and millions of pounds/kilograms

| Washington | New York | Michigan | California | Pennsylvania |
|---|---|---|---|---|
| 4.9 B lbs. 2.2 B kg. | 1.1 B lbs. 500 M kg. | 1.0 B lbs. 450 M kg. | 975 M lbs. 442 M kg. | 475 M lbs. 215 M kg. |

# Washington

# State with the Longest
# Steel Arch Bridge

## West Virginia

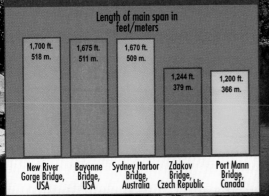

**THE WORLD'S LONGEST STEEL ARCH BRIDGES**

Length of main span in feet/meters

| | | | | |
|---|---|---|---|---|
| 1,700 ft. 518 m. | 1,675 ft. 511 m. | 1,670 ft. 509 m. | 1,244 ft. 379 m. | 1,200 ft. 366 m. |
| New River Gorge Bridge, USA | Bayonne Bridge, USA | Sydney Harbor Bridge, Australia | Zdakov Bridge, Czech Republic | Port Mann Bridge, Canada |

The New River Gorge Bridge in Fayetteville, West Virginia, has a main span of 1,700 feet (518 m) and weighs about 88 million pounds (40 million kg). This makes it not only the largest and longest U.S. steel arch bridge, but also the world's longest. It is approximately 875 feet (267 m) above the New River, and is the second highest bridge in the United States. After three years of construction, the bridge was completed in 1977. This $37-million structure is the focus of Bridge Day—a statewide annual festival that commemorates its building. This is the only day that the New River Gorge Bridge is open to pedestrians.

155

# State With North America's Longest
# Cross-Country Ski Race

The American Birkebeiner cross-country ski marathon is the longest cross-country ski race in North America. The trail winds for 31.7 miles (51 km) through the woods of northern Wisconsin and finishes on Main Street in Hayward. Since it began in 1973, skiers from all parts of the world take part in this event each February. About 6,500 participants and 20,000 spectators are expected for the 2002 "Birkie." Shorter races are also held for younger skiers. On race day, skiers and spectators consume approximately 10,000 oranges, 4,000 cups of hot chocolate, 5,000 gallons of water, and 16,000 cookies.

## Wisconsin

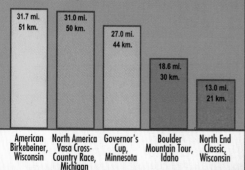

### NORTH AMERICA'S
### LONGEST CROSS-COUNTRY SKI RACES

Length of race in miles/kilometers

| 31.7 mi. 51 km. | 31.0 mi. 50 km. | 27.0 mi. 44 km. | 18.6 mi. 30 km. | 13.0 mi. 21 km. |
|---|---|---|---|---|
| American Birkebeiner, Wisconsin | North America Vasa Cross-Country Race, Michigan | Governor's Cup, Minnesota | Boulder Mountain Tour, Idaho | North End Classic, Wisconsin |

# State with the Oldest National Park

## Wyoming

In March of 1872, the U.S. Congress designated the Yellowstone region of eastern Wyoming as the world's first national park. This giant preserve covers almost 3,470 square miles (8,987 sq km) of mostly undeveloped land. Many geological features found at Yellowstone are unusual. In fact, the park has more than 10,000 hot springs and 200 geysers—the greatest concentration of geothermal features in the world. Yellowstone is also known for its wildlife. Bison, bighorn sheep, moose, black bears, wolves, and many species of birds and fish can be found in the park.

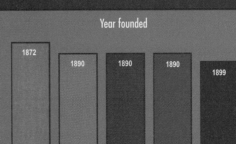

### STATES WITH THE OLDEST NATIONAL PARKS

Year founded

| Yellowstone, Wyoming, Montana, Idaho | Sequoia, California | Kings Canyon, California | Yosemite, California | Mt. Rainier, Washington |
|---|---|---|---|---|
| 1872 | 1890 | 1890 | 1890 | 1899 |

# Science and Technology Records

## Vehicles • Space • Technology
## Video Games • Computers • Solar System

# World's Fastest
# Passenger Train

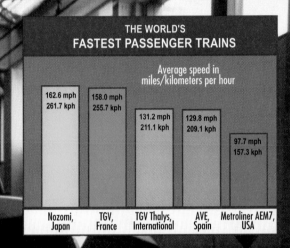

### THE WORLD'S FASTEST PASSENGER TRAINS

Average speed in miles/kilometers per hour

| Nozomi, Japan | TGV, France | TGV Thalys, International | AVE, Spain | Metroliner AEM7, USA |
|---|---|---|---|---|
| 162.6 mph 261.7 kph | 158.0 mph 255.7 kph | 131.2 mph 211.1 kph | 129.8 mph 209.1 kph | 97.7 mph 157.3 kph |

# Nozomi

The Nozomi, which is part of the Japanese 500 design series, carries passengers from Hiroshima to Kokura at an average speed of 162 miles (261 km) per hour. At that speed, the 119-mile (192-km) train ride takes only 44 minutes. The Nozomi also carries passengers for 370 miles (595 km) on the Sanyo Line between Osaka and Hakata, arriving at the station in just 2 hours and 17 minutes. This train was designed by the West Japan Railway Company and is capable of reaching a maximum speed of 186 miles (299 km) per hour.

# World's Largest
# Steem Engine

## 2-6-6-6 Allegheny

When the Chesapeake & Ohio Railroad needed a powerful locomotive to move coal through the Allegheny Mountains, it built the 1.2 million-pound (.54 million-kg) 2-6-6-6 Allegheny in 1941. Although the track was only 80 miles (129 km) long, the company needed a vehicle that could make the 13-mile- (21-km) long climb up a 2,072-foot- (631.5-m) tall mountain while carrying several tons of coal. The 2-6-6-6—which was named for its wheel arrangement—is capable of up to 8,000 horsepower. With one locomotive pulling and the other pushing, this monstrous machine can move 145 cars full of coal.

### SOME OF THE WORLD'S LARGEST STEAM ENGINES

Total weight in millions of pounds/kilograms

| 2-6-6-6 Allegheny | Virginian Blue Ridge | PRR Q2 4-4-6-4 | 6-8-6 Pennsylvania Railroad | 4-6-4 Class 15 |
|---|---|---|---|---|
| 1.20 M lbs. 1.1 M kg. | 1.19 M lbs. 1.08 M kg. | 1.05 M lbs. .953 M kg. | 1.04 M lbs. .94 M kg. | .647 M lbs. .587 M kg. |

# World's Largest Cruise Ship

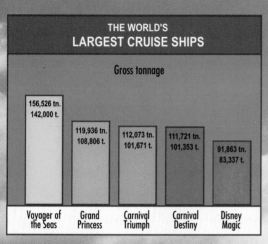

**THE WORLD'S LARGEST CRUISE SHIPS**

Gross tonnage

| Ship | Gross tonnage |
| --- | --- |
| Voyager of the Seas | 156,526 tn. / 142,000 t. |
| Grand Princess | 119,936 tn. / 108,806 t. |
| Carnival Triumph | 112,073 tn. / 101,671 t. |
| Carnival Destiny | 111,721 tn. / 101,353 t. |
| Disney Magic | 91,863 tn. / 83,337 t. |

Royal Caribbean International's *Voyager of the Seas* cruise ship weighs 156,526 tons (142,000 t), which is the equivalent of 313 million pounds (142 million kg). Built in 1999, this giant vessel is also roughly the size of three football fields and is capable of carrying 3,840 passengers and 1,181 crew. It is larger than most hotels. Some of the onboard features include an ice-skating rink, rock climbing wall, street fair, three pools, and a spa. The *Voyager of the Seas* also has 3 dining rooms, 14 passenger elevators, and 3,114 cabins.

# Voyager of the Seas

# World's Fastest Production Car

## Lamborghini Diablo 5.7

This low-lying Italian sports car can reach speeds of more than 200 miles (322 km) per hour. With the ability to go from 0–60 mph in less than 4 seconds, the Lamborghini Diablo has one of the world's most impressive acceleration abilities for a production (mass-produced) vehicle. This two-seater packs a lot of power into a small space, with a V12 engine and 492 horsepower. It was first built in 1995, and today sells for around $250,000—which is about $100,000 higher than the average price of a new house.

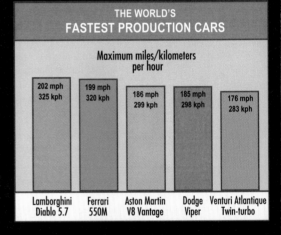

THE WORLD'S FASTEST PRODUCTION CARS

Maximum miles/kilometers per hour

| 202 mph 325 kph | 199 mph 320 kph | 186 mph 299 kph | 185 mph 298 kph | 176 mph 283 kph |
| --- | --- | --- | --- | --- |
| Lamborghini Diablo 5.7 | Ferrari 550M | Aston Martin V8 Vantage | Dodge Viper | Venturi Atlantique Twin-turbo |

# World's Fastest Production Motorcycle

# Suzuki GSX1300R Hayabusa

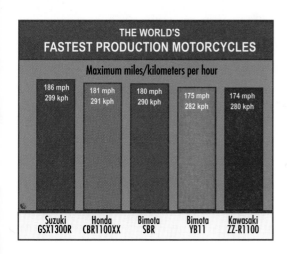

## THE WORLD'S FASTEST PRODUCTION MOTORCYCLES

### Maximum miles/kilometers per hour

| Suzuki GSX1300R | Honda CBR1100XX | Bimota SBR | Bimota YB11 | Kawasaki ZZ-R1100 |
|---|---|---|---|---|
| 186 mph 299 kph | 181 mph 291 kph | 180 mph 290 kph | 175 mph 282 kph | 174 mph 280 kph |

This sleek speed machine, which is named after one of the world's fastest birds, is able to reach a maximum speed of 186 miles (299 km) per hour. That's about three times faster than the speed limit on most major highways. In 1999, the Hayabusa won several major awards, including Motorcycle of the Year and Best Superbike. Its aerodynamic shape, four-cylinder liquid-cooled engine, six-speed transmission, and powerful disc brakes make the bike very popular with motorcycle enthusiasts.

# World's Fastest Land Vehicle

## Thrust SSC

On October 15, 1997, driver Andy Green reached a speed of 763 miles (1,228 km) per hour in the Thrust SSC. At that speed, a car could make it from San Francisco to New York city in less than 4 hours. The Thrust SSC, which stands for SuperSonic Car, is 54 feet (16.5 m) long and weighs 7 tons (6.4 t). It is propelled by two jet engines capable of 110,000 horse-power. The Thrust SSC runs on jet fuel, using about 5 gallons (19 l) per second. It only takes approximately five seconds for this supersonic car to reach its top speed.

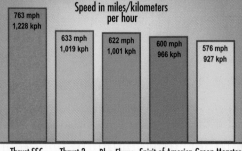

### VEHICLES WITH THE FASTEST SPEED ON LAND

Speed in miles/kilometers per hour

| | | | | |
|---|---|---|---|---|
| 763 mph 1,228 kph | 633 mph 1,019 kph | 622 mph 1,001 kph | 600 mph 966 kph | 576 mph 927 kph |
| Thrust SSC, 1997 | Thrust 2, 1983 | Blue Flame, 1970 | Spirit of America, 1965 | Green Monster, 1965 |

# Fastest Speed on a Boat

317.60 mph

## THE WORLD'S FASTEST BOATS

Average speed in miles/kilometers per hour

| Spirit of Australia, 1978 | Spirit of Australia, 1977 | Hustler, 1967 | Bluebird K7, 1964 | Bluebird K7, 1959 |
|---|---|---|---|---|
| 317.6 mph 511.1 kph | 288.6 mph 464.4 kph | 285.2 mph 458.9 kph | 276.3 mph 444.6 kph | 260.3 mph 418.9 kph |

In October of 1978, Ken Warby averaged 317.60 miles per hour (511.1 kph) in his *Spirit of Australia*—a boat he built himself in his backyard. The speed he reached was nearly as fast as the fastest motorcycle on record. Warby's speed test took place at a .62-mile (1-km) course on the Blowering Dam in New South Wales, Australia. To qualify for the World Water Speed Record, boaters have to make two back-to-back passes over the course and take the average time. The *Spirit of Australia* is permanently displayed at the Australian National Maritime Museum.

# World's Fastest
# Plane

The Lockheed SR-71 Blackbird is capable of flying at a maximum speed of 2,193 miles (3,529 km) per hour. At that rate, the Blackbird could fly from Los Angeles to New York City in just 90 minutes, instead of the average commercial jetliner time of 6 hours. The plane also holds the record for flying at the highest altitude, which is 85,069 feet (25,929 m). The Blackbird measures 107.5 feet (32.8 m) long and has a wingspan of 55.7 feet (17 m). This two-seater plane is manufactured in the United States and has been in service since 1966.

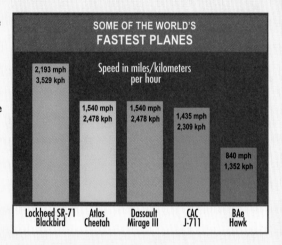

SOME OF THE WORLD'S
**FASTEST PLANES**

Speed in miles/kilometers
per hour

| Plane | Speed |
|---|---|
| Lockheed SR-71 Blackbird | 2,193 mph / 3,529 kph |
| Atlas Cheetah | 1,540 mph / 2,478 kph |
| Dassault Mirage III | 1,540 mph / 2,478 kph |
| CAC J-711 | 1,435 mph / 2,309 kph |
| BAe Hawk | 840 mph / 1,352 kph |

## Lockheed SR-71
## Blackbird

# Largest Human-Made
# Object in Space

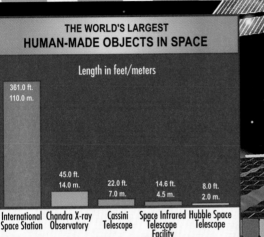

**THE WORLD'S LARGEST HUMAN-MADE OBJECTS IN SPACE**

Length in feet/meters

| Object | Length |
|--------|--------|
| International Space Station | 361.0 ft. / 110.0 m. |
| Chandra X-ray Observatory | 45.0 ft. / 14.0 m. |
| Cassini Telescope | 22.0 ft. / 7.0 m. |
| Space Infrared Telescope Facility | 14.6 ft. / 4.5 m. |
| Hubble Space Telescope | 8.0 ft. / 2.0 m. |

From end to end, the International Space Station will measure 361 feet (110 m) and weigh 460 tons (417 t). The structure's outside surface will be roughly the size of two football fields—the inside will have about the same amount of room as a 747 jumbo jet. The giant space lab will be completed by 2005, after astronauts from several countries assemble the more than 100 sections that make up the craft. A total of 8 miles (12.9 km) of wire will run through the station, feeding 52 onboard computers. It will cost about $100 billion to build and maintain the ISS for the first 10 years.

## International Space Station

# Youngest Astronaut

At age 25, Russian Gherman Stepanovich Titov is the youngest astronaut ever to travel into space. Titov blasted off on August 6, 1961, in a one-person *Vostok 2* spacecraft. He circled Earth for a whole day, orbiting it 17 times. He is the first astronaut to spend a day in space, to sleep in space, and to have motion sickness in space. Titov documented his trip with a movie camera. When Titov landed back on Earth he was named a hero in the Soviet Union.

## Gherman Stepanovich Titov

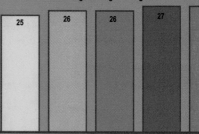

**THE WORLD'S YOUNGEST ASTRONAUTS**

Age during first flight

| Gherman Stepanovich Titov (August 6, 1961) | Valentina V. Tereshkova (June 16, 1963) | Boris B. Yegorov (October 12, 1964) | Yuri A. Gagarin (April 12, 1961) | Janice E. Voss (June 21, 1993) |
|---|---|---|---|---|
| 25 | 26 | 26 | 27 | 27 |

# World's Longest
# Shuttle Flight

## STS-80
## Columbia

During a flight that began on November 19, 1996, the Columbia space shuttle flew for a record 17 days, 15 hours, 53 minutes, and 26 seconds. The Columbia shuttle, which had set the prior flight record four months earlier, was only supposed to be in flight for 15 days. The landing, however, was postponed for two days due to bad weather near the landing pad at Kennedy Space Center. During Columbia's record mission, the crew performed microgravity research and prepared for construction of the International Space Station.

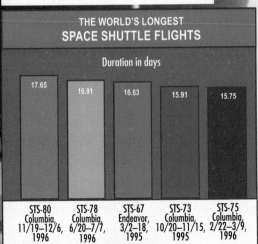

THE WORLD'S LONGEST
## SPACE SHUTTLE FLIGHTS

Duration in days

| STS-80 Columbia, 11/19–12/6, 1996 | STS-78 Columbia, 6/20–7/7, 1996 | STS-67 Endeavor, 3/2–18, 1995 | STS-73 Columbia, 10/20–11/15, 1995 | STS-75 Columbia, 2/22–3/9, 1996 |
|---|---|---|---|---|
| 17.65 | 16.91 | 16.63 | 15.91 | 15.75 |

# World's Largest
# Optical Telescopes

## Keck I / Keck II

The Keck Observatory, located at the top of Mauna Kea on Hawaii, houses two giant optical telescopes—each with a 32.8-foot (10-m) aperture; or opening. Keck I was built in 1992, and Keck II was completed in 1996. Both telescopes stand 8 stories high and weigh 300 tons (272 t). Together, they are operated by the California Institute of Technology and the University of California, Berkeley. The telescopes are powerful enough to identify objects about the size of a penny at a distance of more than 5 miles (8 km) away, and have been used to study the evolution of the universe.

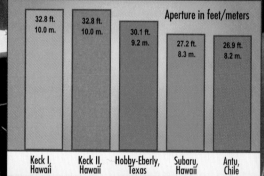

THE WORLD'S
**LARGEST OPTICAL TELESCOPES**

Aperture in feet/meters

| Keck I, Hawaii | Keck II, Hawaii | Hobby-Eberly, Texas | Subaru, Hawaii | Antu, Chile |
|---|---|---|---|---|
| 32.8 ft. 10.0 m. | 32.8 ft. 10.0 m. | 30.1 ft. 9.2 m. | 27.2 ft. 8.3 m. | 26.9 ft. 8.2 m. |

# World's Largest Radio Telescope

## Arecibo

The Arecibo Observatory, located in Puerto Rico, contains the world's largest single-unit radio telescope. This huge instrument houses a sphere reflector that measures 1,000 feet (305 m) long. The reflector is made up of aluminum panels that direct incoming radio waves to antennas located 550 feet (168 m) above the surface of the reflector. The Arecibo radio telescope is operated in conjunction with Cornell University in New York and is used to study planetary radar, pulsars, and other phenomena. It has provided information about the surface of Venus and the planet's rotation.

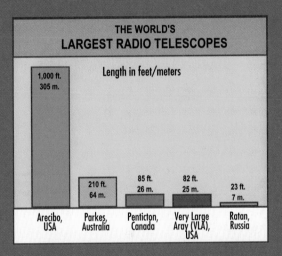

**THE WORLD'S LARGEST RADIO TELESCOPES**

Length in feet/meters

| Telescope | Length |
|---|---|
| Arecibo, USA | 1,000 ft. / 305 m. |
| Parkes, Australia | 210 ft. / 64 m. |
| Penticton, Canada | 85 ft. / 26 m. |
| Very Large Array (VLA), USA | 82 ft. / 25 m. |
| Ratan, Russia | 23 ft. / 7 m. |

# World's
# Heaviest Satellite

The 35,000-pound (15,876-kg) Compton Gamma Ray Observatory (CGRO) was launched into orbit in April of 1991 by the Space Shuttle *Atlantis*. From tip to tip, the observatory measured a total of 70 feet (21 m). The craft orbited approximately 270 miles (435 km) above Earth, and obtained gamma-ray measurements from distant space with 4 special instruments. In June of 2000, scientists dropped the observatory into the Pacific Ocean because they noticed that some of its hardware was not functioning properly. Gamma-ray emissions are studied by scientists so they may better understand the workings of our complex universe.

## THE WORLD'S HEAVIEST SATELLITES

Appproximate weight in pounds/kilograms

|  |  |
|---|---|
| Compton Gamma Ray Observatory | 35,000 lb. 15, 876 kg. |
| Milstar Satellite Communication System | 10,000 lb. 4,536 kg. |
| HS-702 | 9,900 lb. 4,490 kg. |
| HS-601 | 7,716 lb. 3,500 kg. |
| TDRSS | 7,000 lb. 3,175 kg. |

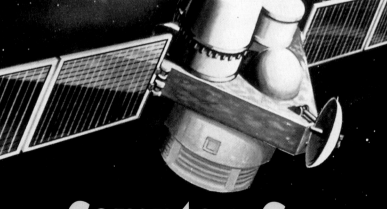

# Compton Gamma
# Ray Observatory

# World's
# Smallest Guitar

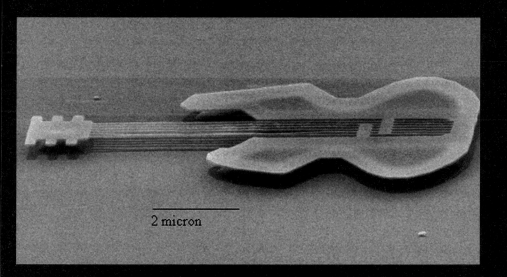

2 micron

# Nanoguitar

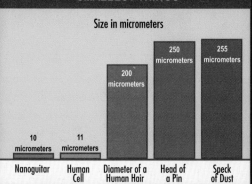

THE WORLD'S
SMALLEST THINGS

Size in micrometers

| Nanoguitar | Human Cell | Diameter of a Human Hair | Head of a Pin | Speck of Dust |
|---|---|---|---|---|
| 10 micrometers | 11 micrometers | 200 micrometers | 250 micrometers | 255 micrometers |

This microscopic musical instrument measures a mere 10 micrometers long—about the same length as a human cell. The guitar has 6 strings that are about 50 nanometers (one-billionth of a meter) wide. If these strings were plucked they would create a sound, but human ears would not be able to hear it. The nanoguitar was created in 1997 from crystalline silicon at Cornell University by Professor Harold Craighead and graduate student Dustin Carr. Its purpose was to demonstrate some new technology that may be used in electronics and fiber optics.

173

# Country with the Most Telephones

Sweden

It seems that people in Sweden like to speak with each other—a lot. For every 10 people living in Sweden, there are almost 9 telephones. That is six times higher than the world average. It means that the country's 8.9 million Swedish residents have access to more than 8.2 million telephones. This high concentration of telephones is not too surprising—Stockholm is a world leader in the production of communications equipment. Sweden also has an excellent domestic and international telephone system.

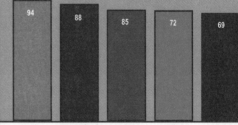

**WORLD COUNTRIES WITH THE MOST TELEPHONES**

Telephones per 100 inhabitants

| Sweden | Switzerland | Denmark | USA | France |
|--------|-------------|---------|-----|--------|
| 94 | 88 | 85 | 72 | 69 |

# Country with the
# Most Cell Phone Users

## Finland

### COUNTRIES WITH THE
### MOST CELL PHONE USERS

Percentage of population using cell phones

| 64% | 61% | 57% | 57% | 53% |
|-----|-----|-----|-----|-----|
| Finland | Norway | Hong Kong | Sweden | Israel |

In Finland, there are more than 3.3 million people using cell phones. That means that about 64% of the population is taking advantage of wireless communication. Reliable and portable communication in Finland is very important for its people. The country is one of the most northern and geographically remote in the world. And although they have a good network of highways, the often harsh weather and lack of direct routes can make travel unpredictable.

175

# Country with the Most TV Sets

# The United States

## COUNTRIES WITH THE MOST TELEVISIONS PER CAPITA

Televisions per 1,000 people

| USA | Canada | Japan | Australia | UK |
|-----|--------|-------|-----------|-----|
| 806 | 709 | 700 | 666 | 612 |

There are approximately 806 television sets for every 1,000 people in the United States. That means there are about 217 million U.S. televisions in use right now. Americans have become addicted to television. The average person living in the United States watches about 1,551 hours of television programming each year. That's equal to nearly 65 straight days, or 18% of one year. Approximately 67% of television owners subscribe to basic cable, which means nearly 70 million viewers have access to a wide range of channels.

# World's Best-Selling
# Video Game

During the 1999 season, Nintendo's Pokémon Blue video game sold more than 6.1 million units. In fact, all Pokémon products were very popular—each of the top five games features the little Pocket Monsters. Players must begin Pokémon Blue by choosing a tame Pokémon from Professor Oak. Each player must train his or her Pokémon to fight and capture other Pokémon. The object is to capture all of the 150 different types of Pokémon. Some rare Pokémon are not in every game, so players must trade the little monsters with one another through Game Boy Paks.

### THE WORLD'S BEST-SELLING VIDEO GAMES

1999 sales in millions of copies

| Pokémon Blue | Pokémon Red | Pokémon Yellow | Pokémon Pinball | Pokémon Snap |
|---|---|---|---|---|
| 6.1 M | 5.8 M | 4.5 M | 3.9 M | 3.7 M |

# Pokémon Blue

# World's Best-Selling
# Video Game Genre

## Strategy

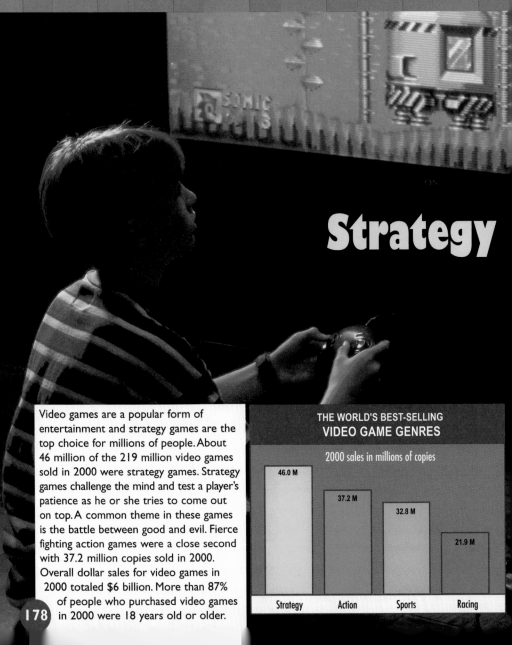

Video games are a popular form of entertainment and strategy games are the top choice for millions of people. About 46 million of the 219 million video games sold in 2000 were strategy games. Strategy games challenge the mind and test a player's patience as he or she tries to come out on top. A common theme in these games is the battle between good and evil. Fierce fighting action games were a close second with 37.2 million copies sold in 2000. Overall dollar sales for video games in 2000 totaled $6 billion. More than 87% of people who purchased video games in 2000 were 18 years old or older.

### THE WORLD'S BEST-SELLING VIDEO GAME GENRES

2000 sales in millions of copies

| Strategy | Action | Sports | Racing |
|----------|--------|--------|--------|
| 46.0 M | 37.2 M | 32.8 M | 21.9 M |

# World's Largest
# Software Company

## Microsoft

International software giant Microsoft, which was started by Bill Gates and Paul Allen in 1975, made an incredible $22.9 billion in 2000. The company name is a combination of the words *microcomputer* and *software*. In addition to software and related applications, Microsoft also provides e-mail services, publishes books, and distributes programming software. The company is based in Redmond, Washington, and went public in 1986. One of Microsoft's most successful products has been its Windows series operating system.

**THE WORLD'S LARGEST SOFTWARE COMPANIES**

Sales, in billions of US dollars

| Company | Sales |
|---|---|
| Microsoft | $22.9 B |
| Oracle | $10.1 B |
| Computer Associates International | $6.1 B |
| Compuware | $2.2 B |
| Siebel Systems | $1.7 B |

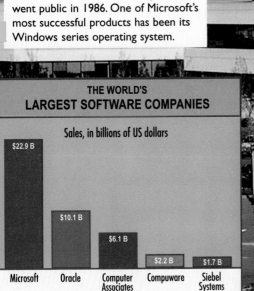

# Country with the Most Computers-in-Use

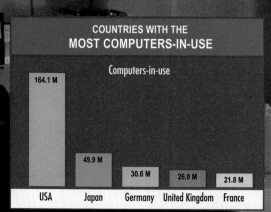
The United States is computer crazy—it has approximately 164 million computers-in-use. That is about 28% of the world total of 579 million computers-in-use. Americans use computers for business and school, to pay bills, send e-mail, and play games. Surfing the World Wide Web is also a popular American pastime. In the next few years, there will be 57 million households connected to the Internet. Many Americans are also shopping on-line, and will spend about $38 billion in 2002.

## The United States

# World's Highest
# Internet Use

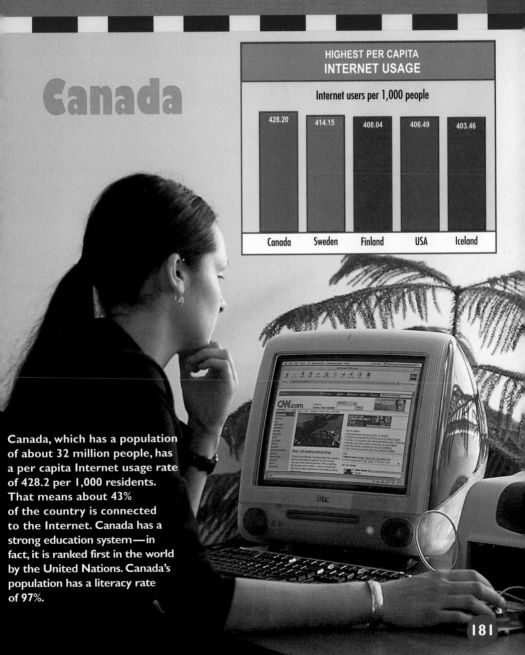

Canada

**HIGHEST PER CAPITA INTERNET USAGE**

Internet users per 1,000 people

| Canada | Sweden | Finland | USA | Iceland |
|--------|--------|---------|-----|---------|
| 428.20 | 414.15 | 408.04 | 406.49 | 403.46 |

Canada, which has a population of about 32 million people, has a per capita Internet usage rate of 428.2 per 1,000 residents. That means about 43% of the country is connected to the Internet. Canada has a strong education system—in fact, it is ranked first in the world by the United Nations. Canada's population has a literacy rate of 97%.

# Country with the Most Internet Users

# The United States

In the United States, almost 135 million people are surfing the World Wide Web. That's about 50% of the population. As more and more services are offered online—everything from banking to grocery shopping to picking out a car—it's not surprising that Internet usage has increased drastically in every age group. Throughout the nation, the largest number of Internet users is women between the ages of 18 and 54, closely followed by men in that age group. Teens aged 12 to 17 are the third-largest Internet-using group.

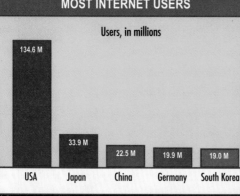

**THE COUNTRIES WITH THE MOST INTERNET USERS**

Users, in millions

| USA | Japan | China | Germany | South Korea |
|-----|-------|-------|---------|-------------|
| 134.6 M | 33.9 M | 22.5 M | 19.9 M | 19.0 M |

# World's Most-Visited Web Site

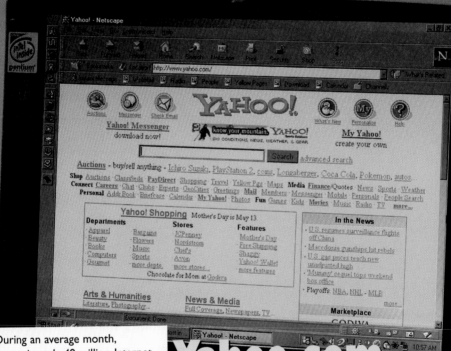

Yahoo.com

During an average month, approximately 49 million Internet users click on a Yahoo! Web page at least once. The Yahoo! site, which first began as a hobby for two young men, has turned into a powerful and extremely popular search engine. Yahoo! was created by David Filo and Jerry Yang in 1994 as a way to keep track of their favorite Web pages. When the site outgrew the storage space of a single computer, the inventors moved their files onto giant computers run by Netscape Communications. The company went public in 1998 with great success and is now worth billions of dollars.

## THE WEB SITES WITH THE MOST VISITORS

Number of new users each month, in millions

| Web Site | New users (millions) |
| --- | --- |
| Yahoo.com | 49.3 M |
| MSN.com | 41.6 M |
| AOL.com | 35.1 M |
| Microsoft.com | 30.0 M |
| Lycos.com | 27.6 M |

# Solar System's
# Largest Planet

## Jupiter

Jupiter has a radius of 43,441 miles (69,909 km)—that's almost 11 times larger than Earth's radius. Although it is very large, Jupiter has a high rotation speed. In fact, one Jupiter day is less than 10 Earth hours long. That is the shortest day in the solar system. Jupiter is about 480 million miles (772 million km) from the Sun. It takes almost 12 Earth years for Jupiter to make one complete circle around the Sun.

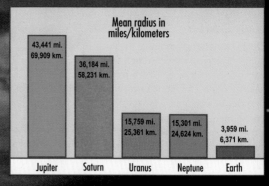

### THE SOLAR SYSTEM'S
### LARGEST PLANETS

Mean radius in miles/kilometers

| Jupiter | Saturn | Uranus | Neptune | Earth |
|---------|--------|--------|---------|-------|
| 43,441 mi. 69,909 km. | 36,184 mi. 58,231 km. | 15,759 mi. 25,361 km. | 15,301 mi. 24,624 km. | 3,959 mi. 6,371 km. |

# Solar System's
# Smallest Planet

## Pluto

Pluto has a radius of about 707 miles (1,138 km). That's about two-thirds the size of the Moon. First noticed in 1930, Pluto was the last planet to be discovered in our solar system. It is normally the farthest planet from the Sun, but its unusual orbit brings it closer than Neptune about every 250 years. The last time this happened was in 1979, when Pluto became the eighth planet for 20 years. Pluto is also the coldest planet, with an average surface temperature of -370° Fahrenheit (-233° Celsius). The planet appears to have polar ice caps that extend halfway to its equator.

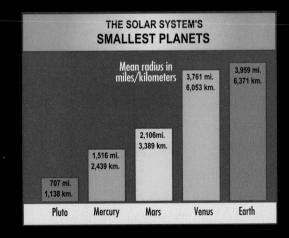

### THE SOLAR SYSTEM'S
### SMALLEST PLANETS

Mean radius in miles/kilometers

| Pluto | Mercury | Mars | Venus | Earth |
|-------|---------|------|-------|-------|
| 707 mi. 1,138 km. | 1,516 mi. 2,439 km. | 2,106 mi. 3,389 km. | 3,761 mi. 6,053 km. | 3,959 mi. 6,371 km. |

*Pluto and its moon, Charon*

# Planet with the Hottest Surface

## Venus

### THE SOLAR SYSTEM'S HOTTEST PLANETS

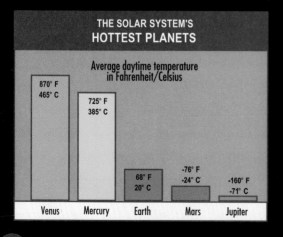

Average daytime temperature in Fahrenheit/Celsius

| Venus | Mercury | Earth | Mars | Jupiter |
|-------|---------|-------|------|---------|
| 870° F<br>465° C | 725° F<br>385° C | 68° F<br>20° C | -76° F<br>-24° C | -160° F<br>-71° C |

The average surface temperature on Venus can reach up to 870° F (465° C). That's about 19 times hotter than the average temperature on Earth. Because Venus is covered by a cloudy, dense atmosphere, it is difficult to know what features are on its surface. This cloud also reflects a great deal of sunlight. At times, Venus is the third-brightest object in the sky, after the Sun and the Moon. About every 19 months, Venus is closer to Earth than any other planet in the solar system.

# Planet with the Most Rings

## Saturn

Scientists estimate that approximately 1,000 rings circle Saturn—hundreds more than any other planet. This ring system reaches a diameter of 167,780 miles (270,000 km), but is only about 328 feet (100 m) thick. Although they appear solid, Saturn's rings are made up of particles of planet and satellite matter that range in size from about 1 to 15 feet (.3 to 4.5 m). The three major rings around the planet are named A, B, and C. Saturn, which is the sixth planet from the Sun, is the solar system's second-largest planet in size and mass.

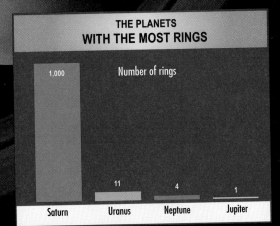

**THE PLANETS WITH THE MOST RINGS**

Number of rings

| Saturn | Uranus | Neptune | Jupiter |
|--------|--------|---------|---------|
| 1,000  | 11     | 4       | 1       |

# Planet with the
# Most Moons

## Saturn

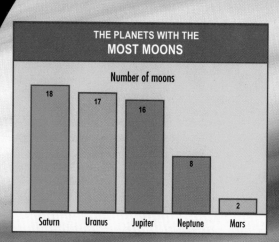

**THE PLANETS WITH THE MOST MOONS**

Number of moons

| Saturn | Uranus | Jupiter | Neptune | Mars |
|--------|--------|---------|---------|------|
| 18 | 17 | 16 | 8 | 2 |

Saturn, the second largest planet in the solar system, has 18 moons—also known as satellites. Eight of these moons were not discovered until 1979. The largest of Saturn's moons is called Titan—it is the only known satellite in the solar system with a dense atmosphere. Saturn's other moons are smaller than Titan and do not have detectable atmospheres. Studies indicate that they are mostly made up of ice. The surfaces of these moons, however, look similar to the rocky surface of Earth's moon.

# Planet with the Fastest Orbit

## Mercury

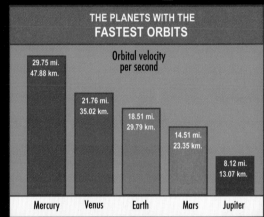

THE PLANETS WITH THE
FASTEST ORBITS

Orbital velocity
per second

| Mercury | Venus | Earth | Mars | Jupiter |
|---------|-------|-------|------|---------|
| 29.75 mi.<br>47.88 km. | 21.76 mi.<br>35.02 km. | 18.51 mi.<br>29.79 km. | 14.51 mi.<br>23.35 km. | 8.12 mi.<br>13.07 km. |

Mercury orbits the Sun with great speed,
averaging about 30 miles (48 km) a second.
At this rate, the planet can circle the Sun in
about 88 Earth days. On Mercury, a solar day
(the time from one sunrise to the next) lasts
about 176 Earth days. Even though Mercury is
the closest planet to the Sun, the temperature
on the planet varies greatly. During the day,
it can reach as high as 840° Fahrenheit
(448° C), but at night temperatures can fall
to around -300° Fahrenheit (-149° C)!

# Planet with the Largest Moon

## Jupiter

Ganymede, the largest moon of both Jupiter and the solar system, has a radius of 1,635 miles (2,631 km) and a diameter of 3,280 miles (5,626 km). That is almost 2.5 times larger than Earth's moon. Ganymede was discovered by Galileo Galilei and Simon Marius almost 400 years ago. It is probably made up mostly of rock and ice. It also has lava flows, mountains, valleys, and craters. Ganymede has both light and dark areas that give it a textured appearance. The moon is approximately 1.4 million miles (2.25 million km) away from Jupiter and has an orbital period of about seven days.

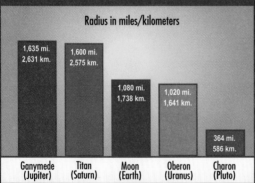

**PLANETS WITH THE LARGEST MOONS**

Radius in miles/kilometers

| Ganymede (Jupiter) | Titan (Saturn) | Moon (Earth) | Oberon (Uranus) | Charon (Pluto) |
|---|---|---|---|---|
| 1,635 mi. 2,631 km. | 1,600 mi. 2,575 km. | 1,080 mi. 1,738 km. | 1,020 mi. 1,641 km. | 364 mi. 586 km. |

# Solar System's
# Brightest Star

## Sirius

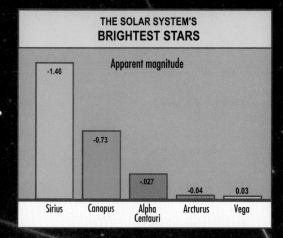

THE SOLAR SYSTEM'S
**BRIGHTEST STARS**

Apparent magnitude

| Sirius | Canopus | Alpha Centauri | Arcturus | Vega |
|--------|---------|----------------|----------|------|
| -1.46 | -0.73 | -.027 | -0.04 | 0.03 |

Star brightness is measured by scientists in something called apparent magnitude. In this measurement system, smaller numbers indicate brighter light. Sirius—also known as the Dog Star or Alpha Canis Majoris—has an apparent magnitude of -1.46, which means it is about 23 times brighter than the Sun. It is also larger and much hotter than the Sun. Sirius was first observed and reported in 1844 by a German astronomer named Friedrich Wilhelm Bessel.

# Solar System's
# Largest Body

# The Sun

The radius of the Sun measures an amazing 432,449 miles (695,940 km) wide—and that's considered small for a star. The Sun's diameter is about 109 times larger than Earth's diameter. The Sun also weighs about 330,000 times more than Earth. In fact, the Sun's mass is 743 times greater than all the planets in the solar system combined. It is so hot on the surface of the Sun that no liquid or solid can exist there, only gas.

**THE SOLAR SYSTEM'S
LARGEST BODIES**

Mean radius in miles/kilometers

| Body | Mean radius |
|------|-------------|
| Sun | 432,449 mi. / 695,940 km. |
| Jupiter | 43,441 mi. / 69,910 km. |
| Saturn | 36,184 mi. / 58,231 km. |
| Uranus | 15,759 mi. / 25,361 km. |
| Neptune | 15,301 mi. / 24,624 km. |

# Money and
# Business Records

**Most Valuable** · **Industry** · **Money**

# World's Most
# Valuable Coin

# Sultan of Muscat
# 1804 Silver Dollar

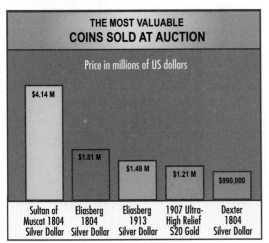

**THE MOST VALUABLE COINS SOLD AT AUCTION**

Price in millions of US dollars

- $4.14 M — Sultan of Muscat 1804 Silver Dollar
- $1.81 M — Eliasberg 1804 Silver Dollar
- $1.48 M — Eliasberg 1913 Silver Dollar
- $1.21 M — 1907 Ultra-High Relief $20 Gold
- $990,000 — Dexter 1804 Silver Dollar

The Sultan of Muscat 1804 Silver Dollar was sold at auction for $4.14 million in New York City on August 30, 1999. One reason for the coin's high value was its mint condition. On a point scale of 1 to 70, it rated a 68. It is also considered to be the best example of that type of coin known today. It is believed to have been given to the Sultan of Muscat as part of a set of proof coins in 1835. Although it's dated 1804, the coin was actually one of only eight silver dollars minted in 1834. They are dated incorrectly because the 1804 coin mold was the only one available.

# World's Most
# Valuable Stamp

# Swedish Treskilling

### THE WORLD'S MOST VALUABLE STAMPS

Estimated worth in US dollars

|  |  |
|---|---|
| Swedish Treskilling | $2.3 M |
| British Guyana 9 | $1.5 M |
| Mauritius 1 | $750,000 |
| Mauritius 2 | $500,000 |
| Hawaii 1 | $250,000 |

The world's rarest stamp, an 1855 Swedish Treskilling Yellow, was sold for $2.3 million in Zurich, Switzerland to an anonymous buyer on November 8, 1996. The reason for the stamp's great value is its extremely rare color. This stamp, which was normally printed in green, was accidentally printed in yellow. Georg Wilhelm Backman first noticed the unusual stamp on a letter at his grandmother's house in 1855. Backman sold it to a stamp dealer a year later, and it continued to increase in value as it changed hands throughout the nineteenth and twentieth centuries.

# World's Most Valuable Barbie®

### THE WORLD'S MOST VALUABLE BARBIE® DOLL

Price in US dollars

| De Beers | Original Prototype | 1959 Ponytail #1, Brunette | 1959 Ponytail #1, Blonde | 1959 Ponytail #2, Brunette |
|---|---|---|---|---|
| $82,870 | $17,000 | $9,500 | $7,500 | $7,000 |

## 40th Anniversary De Beers

To celebrate the fortieth anniversary of Barbie®, the De Beers diamond company helped to create a customized doll worth $82,870. This Barbie® is adorned with 160 diamonds that weigh almost 20 carats, and are set in 18-karat white gold. One fastener on the dress can be removed and worn as a brooch. Even after 40 years in production, the regular Barbie® doll continues to be a worldwide favorite. In fact, there are two dolls sold every second. And to keep her in fashion, Barbie® gets about 120 new outfits each year.

# World's Most
# Valuable Teddy Bear

## Louis Vuitton Steiff Bear

### THE WORLD'S MOST VALUABLE
### TEDDY BEARS SOLD AT AUCTION

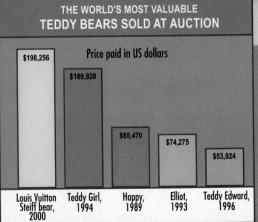

Price paid in US dollars

| | | | | |
|---|---|---|---|---|
| $198,256 | $169,928 | $85,470 | $74,275 | $53,924 |
| Louis Vuitton Steiff bear, 2000 | Teddy Girl, 1994 | Happy, 1989 | Elliot, 1993 | Teddy Edward, 1996 |

At the Teddies de l'An 2000 auction in Monaco in October 2000, a Steiff teddy bear dressed in Louis Vuitton clothes fetched an amazing $198,256. The 17-inch-tall (43-centimeter-tall) bear has jointed arms and legs, and is made of the finest mohair. It is signed by the president of Steiff, and has a special edition ear tag. The Monaco Aide et Presence—the charity that benefited from the auction—and the year 2000 are embroidered on its left foot. Industrialist Jesse Kim bought the bear for his new museum. He hopes to encourage teddy bear collecting in Korea.

# Most Expensive
# Movie Memorabilia

## Judy Garland's Ruby Slippers

**THE WORLD'S MOST EXPENSIVE
MOVIE MEMORABILIA SOLD AT AUCTION**

Price paid in US dollars

| | |
|---|---|
| Judy Garland's Ruby Slippers | $666,000 |
| Vivien Leigh's Gone with the Wind Oscar® | $562,500 |
| Clark Gable's It Happened One Night Oscar® | $507,500 |
| Poster for The Mummy, 1932 | $453,500 |
| James Bond's Aston Martin DB5 | $275,000 |

In May of 2000, the ruby slippers worn by young Dorothy (played by Judy Garland) in *The Wizard of Oz* were auctioned for a record-breaking $666,000 at Christies. There were originally eight pairs of these red satin-and-sequin shoes made for Garland's character, Dorothy Gale, but only four pairs exist today. This particular pair of shoes were also auctioned off in 1988, and brought in $188,000, which was a record at the time. Before they reached Christies, these slippers were on display at Disney's MGM Studio theme park in Orlando, Florida.

# World's Biggest
# Franchise

## McDonald's

There are more than 25,000 McDonald's restaurants in the world, serving customers in 119 different countries. The number of restaurants continues to grow each year by nearly 2,000—that's one new franchise every 5 hours. McDonald's serves about 38 million customers each day, about 20 million of which are in the United States. Out of respect for local cultures, restaurants in different countries modify their menus according to religious or cultural traditions. For example, there is a kosher McDonald's in Jerusalem, and the Big Macs in India are made with lamb instead of beef.

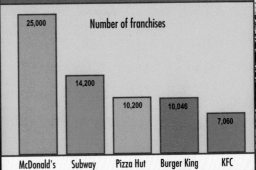

**THE WORLD'S LARGEST INTERNATIONAL FOOD FRANCHISES**

Number of franchises

| McDonald's | Subway | Pizza Hut | Burger King | KFC |
|---|---|---|---|---|
| 25,000 | 14,200 | 10,200 | 10,046 | 7,060 |

# U.S. Company with the Highest Paid CEOs

## Dell Computer

Michael Dell, Chief Executive Officer of Dell Computer, will earn more than $235 million in 2001. Dell founded Dell Computer in 1984 with $1,000 in his pocket and a big idea to start a computer business. Headquartered in Austin, Texas, the company specializes in custom-built computer systems and software. During Michael Dell's 17 years as CEO the company's sales have jumped from $6 million to $32.6 billion. The 36-year-old Dell is worth $16 billion.

**U.S. COMPANIES WITH THE HIGHEST-PAID CEOs**

2001 earnings in millions of US dollars

| Dell Computer | Citigroup | AOL Time Warner | Cisco Systems | Cendant |
|---------------|-----------|-----------------|---------------|---------|
| $235.9 M | $216.1 M | $164.3 M | $157.3 M | $137.4 M |

# The World's Top-Selling Car

## Toyota Corolla

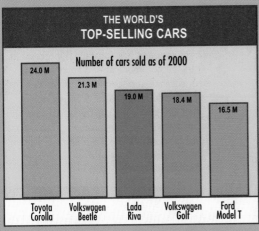

**THE WORLD'S TOP-SELLING CARS**

Number of cars sold as of 2000

| Toyota Corolla | Volkswagen Beetle | Lada Riva | Volkswagen Golf | Ford Model T |
|---|---|---|---|---|
| 24.0 M | 21.3 M | 19.0 M | 18.4 M | 16.5 M |

Since its introduction in 1966, more than 24 million Toyota Corollas have been sold worldwide. The popular Japanese car has developed from a 2-door subcompact to a 4-door sedan. Through the years the Corolla has changed. Air bags were introduced in 1993 and a system was added in 2000 to increase engine power. The first Corolla assembled in the United States rolled out of the factory in 1987, and the 20 millionth Corolla was built in 1997. The Corolla comes in three models—the CE, LE, and sportier S.

# World's Largest Industrial Company

## General Motors

### THE WORLD'S LARGEST INDUSTRIAL COMPANIES

Sales, in billions of US dollars

| General Motors, USA | Wal-Mart Stores, USA | Ford Motor Company, USA | Exxon Mobil, USA | Daimler Chrysler, Germany |
|---|---|---|---|---|
| $176.5 B | $165.0 B | $162.5 B | $160.8 B | $151.6 B |

In 2000, General Motors had $176.5 billion in sales and continued to hold its position as the world's largest automotive corporation. General Motors, which has its headquarters in Detroit, Michigan, mainly designs, manufactures, and markets vehicles and has substantial interests in digital communications, financial and insurance services, locomotives, and heavy-duty automatic transmissions. As the largest U.S. exporter of cars and trucks, GM has manufacturing operations in 50 countries. William Durant, who consolidated several small companies, organized GM in 1908.

# World's
# Largest Bank

The assets for Deutsche Bank totaled $843 billion in 2000. This successful bank was founded in Berlin, Germany in 1870. Today Deutsche Bank's 93,000 employees serve more than 9 million customers throughout the world. There are about 1,500 bank branches located in Germany alone. Deutsche Bank's main services include payments, credit, and personal investment for both private customers and large corporations. The bank also enriches the community by financing music, art, and education projects.

## Deutsche Bank

### THE WORLD'S LARGEST BANKS

Assets, in billions of US dollars

| Deutsche Bank, Germany | Citigroup, USA | BNP Paribas, France | Bank of Tokyo-Mitsubishi Ltd., Japan | Bank of America Corp., USA |
|---|---|---|---|---|
| $843 B | $716 B | $701 B | $697 B | $632 B |

# World's Richest Countries

## Liechtenstein and Switzerland

**THE WORLD'S RICHEST COUNTRIES**

Gross domestic product per capita in US dollars

| Liechtenstein | Switzerland | Japan | Luxembourg | Norway |
|---|---|---|---|---|
| $42,416 | $42,416 | $41,718 | $35,109 | $33,734 |

Liechtenstein and Switzerland are neighboring countries in the middle of Europe. They both have a gross domestic product of $42,416 per capita. The gross domestic product is calculated by dividing the annual worth of all the goods and services produced in a country by that country's population. Even though Liechtenstein is small and has few natural resources, it is home to many successful businesses and industries. This gives the country a high standard of living. Switzerland's excellent economy is the result of a booming export business, an efficient transportation system, and busy tourist industry.

*Liechtenstein*

# World's
# Poorest Country

The Republic of Sudan, located in the northeastern part of Africa, has a gross domestic product of just $36 per capita. The largest country in Africa, Sudan has several reasons for its financial problems. The civil war in Sudan prevents the mass production of oil and gas—a potentially profitable business. Most of the people in sudan earn a living from agriculture, and crop-ruining drought is common. About 30% of the country is unemployed, and inflation has reached 102%.

## The Sudan

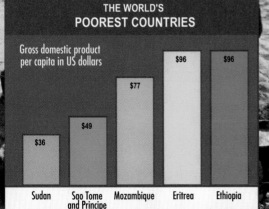

### THE WORLD'S
### POOREST COUNTRIES

Gross domestic product
per capita in US dollars

| Sudan | Sạo Tome and Principe | Mozambique | Eritrea | Ethiopia |
|-------|------------------------|------------|---------|----------|
| $36   | $49                    | $77        | $96     | $96      |

# World's Richest Man

## Bill Gates

Bill Gates is probably one of the world's most recognizable businesspeople. He is the co-founder of Microsoft—the most valuable computer software company in the world—and he is worth an incredible $60 billion. That's enough money to give every person in the world $10. As Microsoft's largest individual shareholder, Gates became a billionaire on paper when the company went public in 1986. Gates' wealth has dropped $30 billion since last year due to a drop in the value of technology stocks.

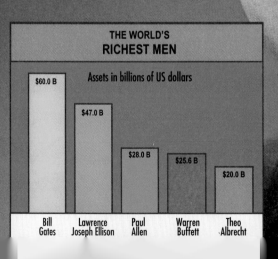

**THE WORLD'S RICHEST MEN**

Assets in billions of US dollars

| | | | | |
|---|---|---|---|---|
| $60.0 B | | | | |
| | $47.0 B | | | |
| | | $28.0 B | $25.6 B | |
| | | | | $20.0 B |
| Bill Gates | Lawrence Joseph Ellison | Paul Allen | Warren Buffett | Theo Albrecht |

# World's RICHEST Women

## Alice and Helen Walton

Helen Walton and her daughter Alice each have an estimated worth of $16 billion. They are two of the heirs to the Walton family fortune, amassed by entrepreneur Sam Walton. He opened the first Wal-Mart store in 1962, and turned it into one of the most successful businesses in American history. Today, Wal-Mart is the world's largest retailer. The Walton Family Foundation was set up as a way for the Waltons to give back to their country. Schools, church groups, community projects, hospitals, and many other organizations throughout the country receive donations.

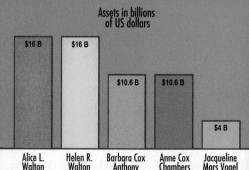

### THE WORLD'S RICHEST WOMEN

Assets in billions of US dollars

| Alice L. Walton | Helen R. Walton | Barbara Cox Anthony | Anne Cox Chambers | Jacqueline Mars Vogel |
|---|---|---|---|---|
| $16 B | $16 B | $10.6 B | $10.6 B | $4 B |

*Helen Walton*

207

# World's Richest Ruler

## King Fahd Bin Abdul-Aziz al-Saud

Fahd Bin Abdul-Aziz al-Saud, the king of Saudi Arabia, is worth approximately $30 billion. That's about 29 times what the queen of England is worth. He was born in Riyadh, Saudia Arabia, in 1923 and is the fifth king of his country. Before taking the throne in 1982, King Fahd became the Minister of Education in 1953. He moved up to the Minister of the Interior in 1962 and held this position for 13 years. Fahd became Crown Prince and the

**THE WORLD'S RICHEST RULERS**

Estimated wealth in billions of US dollars

| | | | | |
|---|---|---|---|---|
| $30 B | | | | |
| | $23 B | | | |
| | | $18 B | | |
| | | | $16 B | |
| | | | | $12 B |
| King Fahd Bin Abdul-Aziz al-Saud, Saudi Arabia | Sheikh Zayed Bin Sultan al-Nahyan, UAE | Jaber al-Ahmed al-Jaber Al-Sabah, Kuwait | Sultan Haji Hassanal Bolkiah, Brunei | Sheikh Maktoum Bin Rashid Al Maktoum, UAE |

# World's All-Time Richest Person

# John D. Rockefeller

In current U.S. dollars, John D. Rockefeller's 1913 fortune of $900 million would be worth about $189 billion. Rockefeller made his money from the Standard Oil Company, which he co-founded in 1870. By 1911, he controlled most of the oil production and transportation industries in the United States. One of the nation's leading philanthropists, Rockefeller was quite generous with his money and donated more than $500 million during his lifetime. His son, John Rockefeller, Jr., donated about $2.5 billion of the family fortune to charitable causes.

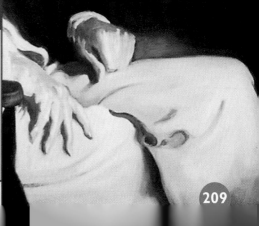

## THE WORLD'S RICHEST PEOPLE OF ALL TIME

Estimated wealth in current billions of US dollars

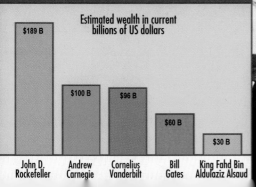

|  |  |
| --- | --- |
| John D. Rockefeller | $189 B |
| Andrew Carnegie | $100 B |
| Cornelius Vanderbilt | $96 B |
| Bill Gates | $60 B |
| King Fahd Bin Aldulaziz Alsaud | $30 B |

# World's Youngest Billionaire

## Athina Onassis Roussel

Greek shipping tycoon Aristotle Onassis left his granddaughter well provided for. When Athina Onassis Roussel turns 18 years old in 2003, she will be worth approximately $2.4 billion. She became the only heir to the Onassis shipping fortune when her mother, Christina, died in 1988. Currently, the estate is being managed by financial advisers. Athina lives in a small village near Lausanne, Switzerland, with her father, Thierry Roussel, and her stepfamily.

She speaks fluent English, French, and Swedish, and enjoys playing sports and horseback riding.

**THE WORLD'S YOUNGEST BILLIONAIRES**

Age in 2002

| Athina Onassis Roussel | Daniel Morton Ziff | Robert David Ziff | Michael Dell | Ted Waitt |
|---|---|---|---|---|
| 17 | 29 | 35 | 36 | 37 |

# Sports
# Records

**Baseball • Basketball • Car Racing • Football • Golf
Hockey • Olympics • Running • Skating • Soccer • Tennis**

# Most MVP Awards in the National League

## Barry Bonds, Roy Campanella, Stan Musial, and Mike Schmidt

During their professional careers in the National Baseball League, Barry Bonds, Roy Campanella, Stan Musial, and Mike Schmidt each won three Most Valuable Player awards. Out of those four players, the only ones to win the awards back-to-back were Barry Bonds (1992-1993) and Mike Schmidt (1980-1981). At the time that they received their MVP awards, both players were with Pennsylvania teams—Bonds with the Pirates and Schmidt with the Phillies. Roy Campanella was a catcher for the Brooklyn Dodgers and Stan Musial was an outfielder for the St. Louis Cardinals.

### PLAYERS WITH THE MOST NATIONAL LEAGUE MVP AWARDS

Most Valuable Player (MVP) awards

| Barry Bonds, 1986— | Roy Campanella, 1948–1957 | Stan Musial, 1941–1963 | Mike Schmidt, 1972–1989 | Ernie Banks, 1953–1971 |
|---|---|---|---|---|
| 3 | 3 | 3 | 3 | 2 |

*Mike Schmidt*

# Most MVP Awards in the American League

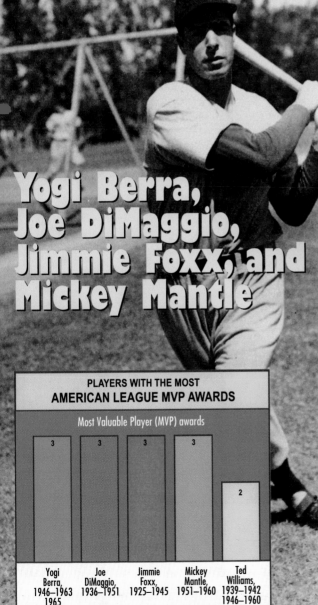

## Yogi Berra, Joe DiMaggio, Jimmie Foxx, and Mickey Mantle

Yogi Berra, Joe DiMaggio, Jimmie Foxx, and Mickey Mantle each won three Most Valuable Player awards during their professional careers in the American Baseball League. The player with the biggest gap between wins was DiMaggio, who won his first award in 1939 and his last in 1947. Also nicknamed "Joltin' Joe" and the "Yankee Clipper," DiMaggio began playing in the major leagues in 1936. The following year, he led the league in home runs and runs scored. He was elected to the Baseball Hall of Fame in 1955. DiMaggio, Berra, and Mantle were all New York Yankees. Foxx played for the Athletics, the Cubs, and the Phillies.

### PLAYERS WITH THE MOST AMERICAN LEAGUE MVP AWARDS

Most Valuable Player (MVP) awards

| Yogi Berra, 1946–1963 1965 | Joe DiMaggio, 1936–1951 | Jimmie Foxx, 1925–1945 | Mickey Mantle, 1951–1960 | Ted Williams, 1939–1942 1946–1960 |
|---|---|---|---|---|
| 3 | 3 | 3 | 3 | 2 |

Joe DiMaggio

213

# World's All-Time
# Home Run Hitter

## Hank Aaron

In 1974, Hank Aaron broke Babe Ruth's lifetime record of 714 home runs. By the time he retired from baseball in 1976, Aaron had hit a total of 755 homers—a record that has remained unbroken. Aaron holds many other distinguished baseball records, including most lifetime runs batted in (2,297) and most years with 30 or more home runs (15).

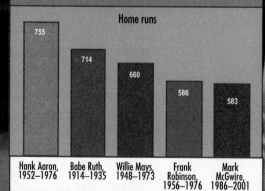

**WORLD'S TOP 5 ALL-TIME HOME RUN HITTERS**

Home runs

| | | | | |
|---|---|---|---|---|
| 755 | 714 | 660 | 586 | 583 |
| Hank Aaron, 1952–1976 | Babe Ruth, 1914–1935 | Willie Mays, 1948–1973 | Frank Robinson, 1956–1976 | Mark McGwire, 1986–2001 |

# Highest Seasonal
# Home Run Total

## Barry Bonds

### BASEBALL'S TOP SEASONAL
### HOME RUN HITTERS

Number of home runs

| 73 | 70 | 66 | 65 | 64 |
|----|----|----|----|----|
| Barry Bonds, 2001 | Mark McGwire, 1998 | Sammy Sosa, 1998 | Mark McGwire, 1999 | Sammy Sosa, 2001 |

Barry Bonds smashed Mark McGwire's record for seasonal home runs when he hit his 71st home run on October 5, 2001, in the first inning of a game against the Los Angeles Dodgers. Two innings later, he hit number 72. Bonds, a left fielder for the San Francisco Giants, has a career total of 567 home runs. He also holds the records for seasonal walks (177) and seasonal slugging percentage (0.863). Bonds was named the National League's Most Valuable Player in 1990, 1992, and 1993.

215

# Most
# Career Hits

## Pete Rose

By the time Pete Rose retired as a player from Major League Baseball in 1986, he had set several career records. During his 23 years of professional baseball, Rose belted an amazing 4,256 hits. He got his record-setting hit in 1985, when he was a player-manager for the Cincinnati Reds. Rose also holds the Major League records for the most career games (3,562), the most times at bat (14,053), and the most seasons with more than 200 hits (10). During his career, he played for the Cincinnati Reds, the Philadelphia Phillies, and the Montreal Expos.

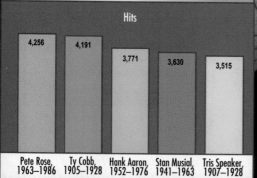

**PLAYERS WITH THE**
**MOST CAREER HITS**

Hits

| Player | Hits |
|---|---|
| Pete Rose, 1963–1986 | 4,256 |
| Ty Cobb, 1905–1928 | 4,191 |
| Hank Aaron, 1952–1976 | 3,771 |
| Stan Musial, 1941–1963 | 3,630 |
| Tris Speaker, 1907–1928 | 3,515 |

# Most
# Career Strikeouts

## Nolan Ryan

Nolan Ryan, a right-handed pitcher from Refugio, Texas, leads Major League Baseball with an incredible 5,714 career strikeouts. During his impressive 28-year career, he led the American League in strikeouts 10 times. In 1989, at the age of 42, Ryan became the oldest pitcher ever to lead the Major League in strikeouts. Ryan also set another record in 1991 when he pitched his seventh career no-hitter. During his time in professional baseball, he played for the New York Mets, the California Angels, the Houston Astros, and the Texas Rangers.

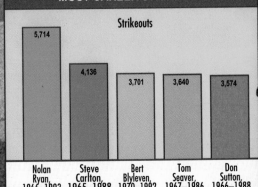

PLAYERS WITH THE
MOST CAREER STRIKEOUTS

Strikeouts

| Nolan Ryan, 1966–1993 | Steve Carlton, 1965–1988 | Bert Blyleven, 1970–1992 | Tom Seaver, 1967–1986 | Don Sutton, 1966–1988 |
|---|---|---|---|---|
| 5,714 | 4,136 | 3,701 | 3,640 | 3,574 |

# Highest Seasonal
# Batting Average

## Rogers Hornsby

In 1924, Rogers Hornsby had a record-setting season batting average of .424. More than 75 years later, his record still stands. From 1921 to 1925—playing for the St. Louis Cardinals—Hornsby hit an average of .401. And during three of those seasons, he hit above .400. He is widely considered by most people to be Major League Baseball's greatest right-handed hitter. Hornsby's major league lifetime batting average is an incredible .358, which is the second-highest career average in the history of the league after Ty Cobb. Hornsby was inducted to the Baseball Hall of Fame in 1942.

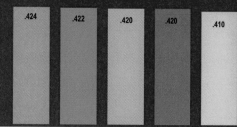

**PLAYERS WITH THE
HIGHEST SEASONAL BATTING AVERAGE**

Season average

| .424 | .422 | .420 | .420 | .410 |
|------|------|------|------|------|
| Rogers Hornsby, 1924 | Nap Lajoie, 1901 | George Sisler, 1922 | Ty Cobb, 1911 | Ty Cobb, 1912 |

# Highest Lifetime
# Slugging Average

## Babe Ruth

The legendary George Herman "Babe" Ruth has the highest lifetime slugging average with an amazing .690. He also holds the lifetime records for home run percentages (8.5%) and walks (2,056). Ruth began his career in 1914 as a left-handed pitcher for the Boston Red Sox. During his twenty complete seasons, he held the league record in home runs 12 times, the record for runs 8 times, the record for runs batted-in 6 times, and the slugging record 13 times. In 1936, Ruth was one of the first five players elected to the Baseball Hall of Fame.

### BASEBALL'S TOP CAREER SLUGGING AVERAGES

Averages

| Babe Ruth, 1914–1935 | Ted Williams, 1939–1942 1946–1960 | Lou Gehrig, 1923–1939 | Jimmie Foxx, 1925–1945 | Hank Greenberg, 1933–1941 1945–1947 |
|---|---|---|---|---|
| .690 | .634 | .632 | .609 | .605 |

219

# World's Longest
# Baseball Game

## Brooklyn Dodgers vs. Boston Braves, May 1, 1920

On May 1, 1920, the Brooklyn Dodgers and the Boston Braves played baseball for 26 consecutive innings, unsuccessfully trying to break a 1-1 tied game. The game lasted just under four hours, and was ended by officials only because it became too dark to see the ball. Amazingly, the pitchers for both teams played the entire game. In fact, Braves pitcher Joe Oeschger shut out the Dodgers for the last 21 innings, setting a record for the most consecutive scoreless innings in baseball history.

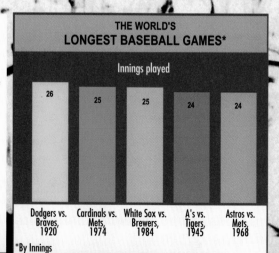

**THE WORLD'S LONGEST BASEBALL GAMES***

Innings played

| | | | | |
|---|---|---|---|---|
| 26 | 25 | 25 | 24 | 24 |
| Dodgers vs. Braves, 1920 | Cardinals vs. Mets, 1974 | White Sox vs. Brewers, 1984 | A's vs. Tigers, 1945 | Astros vs. Mets, 1968 |

*By Innings

# Player Who Played the Most Consecutive Games

## Cal Ripken, Jr.

Cal Ripken, Jr., a right-handed third baseman for the Baltimore Orioles, played 2,632 consecutive games from May 30, 1982 to September 20, 1998. He also holds the record for the most consecutive innings played: 8,243. When he played as a shortstop, Ripken set Major League records for most home runs (345) and most extra base hits (855) for his position. He has started in the All-Star Game a record 19 times in a row, and tied Rod Carew for the most All-Star elections. Ripken has received many awards, including two **MVP** awards and eight Silver Slugger awards.

### PLAYERS WITH THE MOST CONSECUTIVE GAMES PLAYED

Consecutive games played

| Cal Ripken, Jr., 1978–2001 | Lou Gehrig, 1923–1939 | Everett Scott, 1914–1925 | Steve Garvey, 1968–1988 | Billy Williams, 1959–1974 |
|---|---|---|---|---|
| 2,632 | 2,130 | 1,307 | 1,207 | 1,117 |

# Most
# Cy Young Awards

Roger Clemens, currently a right-handed starting pitcher for the New York Yankees, has earned a record six Cy Young awards during his career so far. He has also earned an MVP award, two pitching Triple Crowns, and played in the All-Star Game eight times. He set a Major League Record in April of 1986 when he struck out 20 batters in one game. He later tied this record in September of 1996. In September 2001, Clemens became the first Major League pitcher to win 20 of his first 21 decisions in one season.

## PITCHERS WITH THE
## MOST CY YOUNG AWARDS

Cy Young Awards

| Roger Clemens, 1984– | Steve Carlton, 1965–1988 | Greg Maddux, 1986– | Sandy Koufax, 1955–1966 | Jim Palmer, 1965–1984 |
|---|---|---|---|---|
| 6 | 4 | 4 | 3 | 3 |

# Roger
# Clemens

# Team with the Most
# World Series Wins

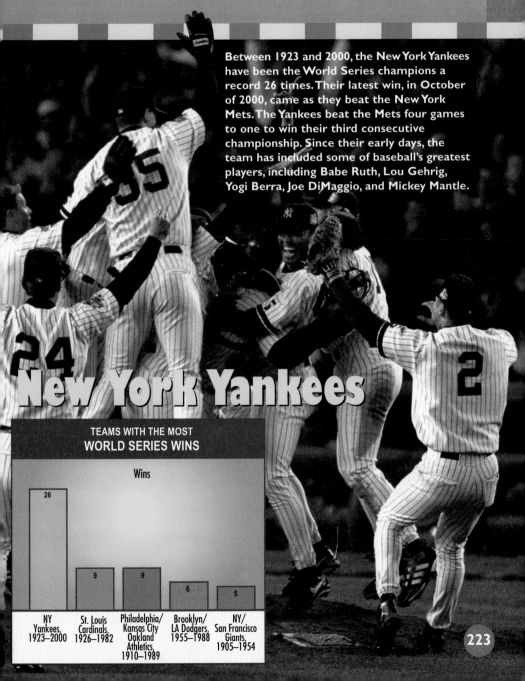

Between 1923 and 2000, the New York Yankees have been the World Series champions a record 26 times. Their latest win, in October of 2000, came as they beat the New York Mets. The Yankees beat the Mets four games to one to win their third consecutive championship. Since their early days, the team has included some of baseball's greatest players, including Babe Ruth, Lou Gehrig, Yogi Berra, Joe DiMaggio, and Mickey Mantle.

## New York Yankees

### TEAMS WITH THE MOST WORLD SERIES WINS

**Wins**

| Team | Wins |
|------|------|
| NY Yankees, 1923–2000 | 26 |
| St. Louis Cardinals, 1926–1982 | 9 |
| Philadelphia/ Kansas City Oakland Athletics, 1910–1989 | 9 |
| Brooklyn/ LA Dodgers, 1955–1988 | 6 |
| NY/ San Francisco Giants, 1905–1954 | 5 |

# Player with the
# Most Career RBIs

## Hank Aaron

### PLAYERS WITH THE
### MOST CAREER RBIs

Runs batted in

| Hank Aaron, 1952–1976 | Babe Ruth, 1914–1935 | Lou Gehrig, 1923–1939 | Ty Cobb, 1905–1928 | Stan Musial, 1941–1963 |
|---|---|---|---|---|
| 2,297 | 2,211 | 1,990 | 1,961 | 1,951 |

During his 23 years in the major leagues, right-handed Hank Aaron batted in an incredible 2,297 runs. In 1952, Aaron began his professional career with the Indianapolis Clowns, a team in the Negro American League. He was later traded to the Atlanta Braves, and in 1956, won the National League batting championship with an average of .328. A year later, he was named the league's Most Valuable Player when he led his team to a World Series victory. Aaron retired as a player in 1976 and was inducted into the Baseball Hall of Fame in 1982.

# Most Career Field Goals

Born Lew Alcindor, Kareem Abdul-Jabbar changed his name when he converted to Islam in 1971. An all-around great player, Abdul-Jabbar holds many NBA distinctions. By the end of his 20-year-long career, Abdul-Jabbar had scored a record 15,837 field goals. He was a member of six championship teams, as well as a member of the NBA's Thirty-fifth and Fiftieth Anniversary All-Time Teams. He was chosen as the NBA's MVP a record six times, and was named NBA Finals MVP twice.

# Kareem Abdul-Jabbar

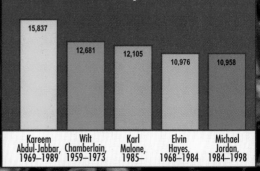

**PLAYERS WITH THE MOST CAREER FIELD GOALS**

Field goals

| Kareem Abdul-Jabbar, 1969–1989 | Wilt Chamberlain, 1959–1973 | Karl Malone, 1985– | Elvin Hayes, 1968–1984 | Michael Jordan, 1984–1998 |
|---|---|---|---|---|
| 15,837 | 12,681 | 12,105 | 10,976 | 10,958 |

# Highest Career
## Scoring Average

Michael
Jordan

Few fans dispute the fact that Michael Jordan is basketball's greatest all-time player. During his career, he averaged an amazing 31.5 points per game. After being named Rookie of the Year in his first NBA season (1984), Jordan led the league in scoring for the next seven years. During the 1986 season, he became the second person ever to score 3,000 points in a single season. Jordan retired from playing basketball in 1998. However, in September 2001, he announced that he would return as a player for the Washington Wizards.

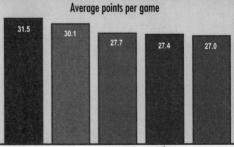

### PLAYERS WITH THE HIGHEST CAREER SCORING AVERAGES

Average points per game

| Michael Jordan, 1984–1998 | Wilt Chamberlain, 1959–1973 | Shaquille O'Neal, 1992– | Elgin Baylor, 1958–1971 | Jerry West, 1960–1972 |
|---|---|---|---|---|
| 31.5 | 30.1 | 27.7 | 27.4 | 27.0 |

# Most Career
## Games Played

# Robert Parish

Robert Parish played in a total of 1,611 NBA games during his 21-year-long career. Parish was a first-round draft pick by the Golden State Warriors in 1976. He went on to win three championships with the Boston Celtics and one with the Chicago Bulls. Parish has played in nine NBA All-Star games and was honored as one of the 50 Greatest Players in NBA History during the 1996–1997 season. By the time he retired in 1997, Parish had scored an astounding 23,334 points and grabbed 14,715 rebounds.

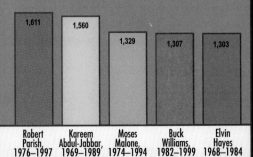

### PLAYERS WITH THE MOST GAMES PLAYED

Games played

| Robert Parish, 1976–1997 | Kareem Abdul-Jabbar, 1969–1989 | Moses Malone, 1974–1994 | Buck Williams, 1982–1999 | Elvin Hayes 1968–1984 |
|---|---|---|---|---|
| 1,611 | 1,560 | 1,329 | 1,307 | 1,303 |

# WNBA Player with the
# Most Career Points

## Lisa Leslie

As a center for the Los Angeles Sparks, Lisa Leslie has scored 2,670 points. Leslie has a career average of 17.7 points per game. She was named MVP of the WNBA All-Star games in 1999 and 2001. Leslie was also a member of the 1996 and 2000 Olympic gold medal-winning women's basketball teams. In 2001, Leslie led her team to victory in the WNBA championship and was named the league's MVP.

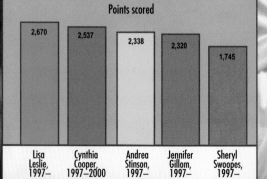

**WNBA PLAYERS WITH THE MOST CAREER POINTS**

Points scored

| Lisa Leslie, 1997– | Cynthia Cooper, 1997–2000 | Andrea Stinson, 1997– | Jennifer Gillom, 1997– | Sheryl Swoopes, 1997– |
|---|---|---|---|---|
| 2,670 | 2,537 | 2,338 | 2,320 | 1,745 |

# Most Career Points

## Kareem Abdul-Jabbar

Kareem Abdul-Jabbar scored a total of 38,387 points during his highly successful career. Abdul-Jabbar began his NBA tenure with the Milwaukee Bucks in 1969 and was named Rookie of the Year in 1970. The following year, he helped the Bucks win the NBA championship by scoring 2,596 points. After he was traded to the Los Angeles Lakers in 1975, he helped that team win the NBA championship in 1980, 1982, 1985, 1987, and 1988. He retired from basketball in 1989 and was inducted into the Basketball Hall of Fame in 1995.

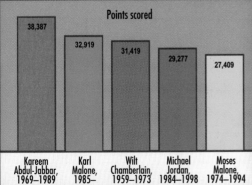

### PLAYERS WITH THE MOST CAREER POINTS

Points scored

| Kareem Abdul-Jabbar, 1969–1989 | Karl Malone, 1985– | Wilt Chamberlain, 1959–1973 | Michael Jordan, 1984–1998 | Moses Malone, 1974–1994 |
|---|---|---|---|---|
| 38,387 | 32,919 | 31,419 | 29,277 | 27,409 |

# Most Career
# Free Throws

As a starter forward for the Utah Jazz, Karl "the Mailman" Malone has made 8,636 free throws. He is second in the NBA in most career points, with 32,919. Malone is only the third player in NBA history to score more than 30,000 points. The Utah Jazz star holds the NBA record for most consecutive seasons scoring 2,000 points or more (1987–1988 to 1997–1998). Malone was named the NBA's most valuable player for the 1996–1997 and 1998–1999 seasons. He was a member of the men's basketball "Dream Teams," that won the gold medal at the 1992 Olympic Games in Barcelona, Spain, and the gold medal at the 1996 Olympics in Atlanta.

# Karl
# Malone

## PLAYERS WITH THE
## MOST CAREER FREE THROWS

### Free throws

| Karl Malone, 1985– | Moses Malone, 1974–1994 | Oscar Robertson, 1960–1972 | Jerry West, 1960–1972 | Dolph Schayes, 1949–1964 |
|---|---|---|---|---|
| 8,636 | 8,531 | 7,694 | 7,160 | 6,979 |

# Most Career
# Rebounds

Wilt Chamberlain—nicknamed "The Big Dipper" and "Wilt the Stilt"—had a record-breaking career average of 22.9 rebounds per game. He also set several other records during his time in the NBA, including one for the most rebounds in a game in 1960, when he made 55 rebounds. Before joining the NBA in 1959, Chamberlain was a Harlem Globetrotter for a year. He later played for the Philadelphia Warriors, the Philadelphia 76ers, and the Los Angeles Lakers. Chamberlain retired in 1973 and was inducted into the Hall of Fame in 1978.

# Wilt
# Chamberlain

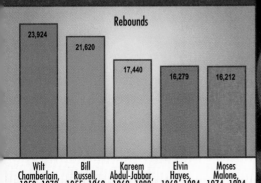

## PLAYERS WITH THE
## MOST CAREER REBOUNDS

Rebounds

| Player | Rebounds |
| --- | --- |
| Wilt Chamberlain, 1959–1973 | 23,924 |
| Bill Russell, 1955–1969 | 21,620 |
| Kareem Abdul-Jabbar, 1969–1989 | 17,440 |
| Elvin Hayes, 1968–1984 | 16,279 |
| Moses Malone, 1974–1994 | 16,212 |

# Player with the Most MVP Awards

## Kareem Abdul-Jabbar

With six Most Valuable Player awards, Kareem Abdul-Jabbar is considered by most people to be one of the greatest players ever to play basketball. He was also an **NBA Finals MVP** twice. He holds many impressive records, including the most blocked shots. Abdul-Jabbar, a 7-foot-tall (2.1 m) center, scored double figures in an amazing 787 straight games. During his 20-year career, this basketball legend played 1,560 games, averaging 24.6 points and 11.2 rebounds a game.

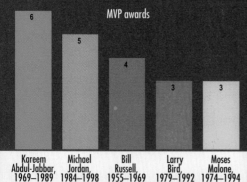

**PLAYERS WITH THE MOST MVP AWARDS**

MVP awards

| Kareem Abdul-Jabbar, 1969–1989 | Michael Jordan, 1984–1998 | Bill Russell, 1955–1969 | Larry Bird, 1979–1992 | Moses Malone, 1974–1994 |
|---|---|---|---|---|
| 6 | 5 | 4 | 3 | 3 |

# Fastest Race Time in the Indianapolis 500

## Arie Luyendyk

### DRIVERS WITH THE FASTEST
### INDIANAPOLIS 500 RACE TIMES

Race times in hours, minutes, and seconds

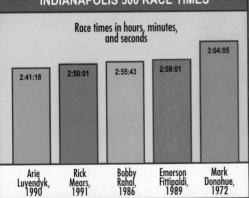

| Arie Luyendyk, 1990 | Rick Mears, 1991 | Bobby Rahal, 1986 | Emerson Fittipaldi, 1989 | Mark Donohue, 1972 |
|---|---|---|---|---|
| 2:41:18 | 2:50:01 | 2:55:43 | 2:59:01 | 3:04:05 |

In 1990, Arie Luyendyk finished the Indianapolis 500 with a world record time of 2 hours, 41 minutes, and 18 seconds. That means he drove the entire race at an average speed of 186 miles (299 km) per hour. That's almost three times faster than the speed limit on most U.S. highways. The record-breaking win was his second Indy 500 victory—he also won in 1997. Luyendyk began racing in his native Netherlands, and competed in his first Indy 500 race in 1985. That year, he finished seventh and was awarded Rookie of the Year. He retired from racing in May 1999.

# Most Victories in the Indianapolis 500

## A.J. Foyt Jr., Rick Mears, and Al Unser

Three of professional car racing's greatest drivers—Rick Mears, A.J. Foyt Jr., and Al Unser—have each won the Indianapolis 500 a total of four times. Of the three champion drivers, Rick Mears had the fastest time with 2 hours, 50 minutes, and 1 second in 1991. Amazingly, one of Mears's Indy 500 victories was only his second Indy race. The Indianapolis 500 began in 1911 in an effort to ban racing from public roads. It is held on the Indianapolis Motor Speedway, on a 2.5-mile- (4-km) long oval track. The Indy 500 is still considered the most prestigious event in all of professional racing.

### DRIVERS WHO HAVE THE MOST INDIANAPOLIS 500 VICTORIES

Number of Indianapolis 500 races won

| A.J. Foyt Jr., 1960–1981 | Rick Mears, 1977–1994 | Al Unser, 1965–1987 | Johnny Rutherford, 1963–1988 | Bobby Unser, 1963–1981 |
|---|---|---|---|---|
| 4 | 4 | 4 | 3 | 3 |

*Rick Mears*

# Most Wins in the Daytona 500

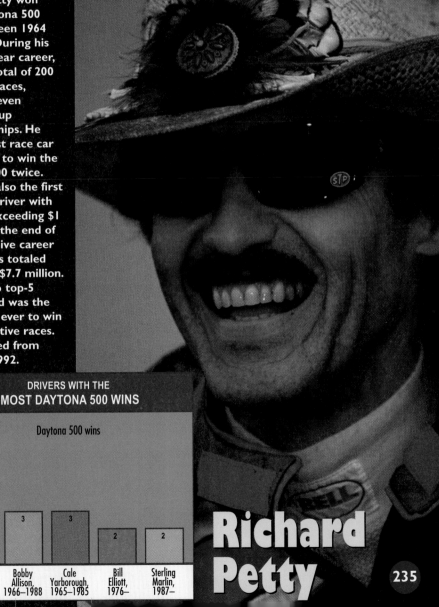

Richard Petty won seven Daytona 500 races between 1964 and 1981. During his entire 34-year career, he won a total of 200 NASCAR races, including seven Winston Cup championships. He was the first race car driver ever to win the Daytona 500 twice. Petty was also the first stock-car driver with winnings exceeding $1 million. By the end of his impressive career his earnings totaled more than $7.7 million. He had 356 top-5 finishes, and was the first driver ever to win 0 consecutive races. Petty retired from racing in 1992.

## DRIVERS WITH THE MOST DAYTONA 500 WINS

Daytona 500 wins

| Richard Petty, 1958–1992 | Bobby Allison, 1966–1988 | Cale Yarborough, 1965–1985 | Bill Elliott, 1976– | Sterling Marlin, 1987– |
|---|---|---|---|---|
| 7 | 3 | 3 | 2 | 2 |

**Richard Petty**

235

# Top Male World-Champion
# Figure Skaters

## Kurt Browning, Scott Hamilton, and Hayes Jenkins

Kurt Browning, Scott Hamilton, and Hayes Jenkins each won 4 world championship competitions during their careers. Browning is from Canada, and was inducted into the Canadian Sports Hall of Fame in 1994. Hamilton and Jenkins are from the United States. Hamilton, who won the competitions from 1981 to 1984, is known for promoting the athleticism in his sport. He also won a gold medal in the 1984 Olympics, and later received the first Olympic Spirit Award in 1987. Jenkins impressive skating career included winning every major championship between 1953 and 1956.

**MEN WITH THE MOST**
**WORLD FIGURE-SKATING CHAMPIONSHIPS**

World figure skating championship wins

| Kurt Browning, Canada, 1989–1993 | Scott Hamilton, USA, 1981–1984 | Hayes Jenkins, USA, 1953–1956 | David Jenkins, USA, 1957–1959 | Elvis Stoyko, Canada, 1994–1997 |
|---|---|---|---|---|
| 4 | 4 | 4 | 3 | 3 |

*Scott Hamilton*

# Top Female World-Champion Figure Skater

## Carol Heiss

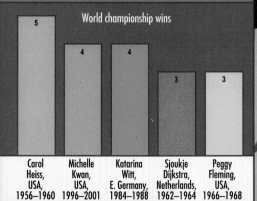

Carol Heiss, an American figure skater, won the Woman's World Figure Skating championships five times between 1956 and 1960. She also won an Olympic silver medal for women's figure skating in 1956, and then a gold medal during the 1960 Winter Olympics in Squaw Valley, California. Heiss turned professional in 1961 and married fellow Olympic skater Hayes Jenkins (who holds a comparable record for most male world championships). She has been inducted into the International Women's Sports Hall of Fame and continues to coach ice skating in Ohio.

### WOMEN WITH THE MOST WORLD FIGURE-SKATING CHAMPIONSHIP WINS

World championship wins

| Carol Heiss, USA, 1956–1960 | Michelle Kwan, USA, 1996–2001 | Katarina Witt, E. Germany, 1984–1988 | Sjoukje Dijkstra, Netherlands, 1962–1964 | Peggy Fleming, USA, 1966–1968 |
|---|---|---|---|---|
| 5 | 4 | 4 | 3 | 3 |

# Highest Career
# Quarterback Rating

## Steve Young

Steve Young holds the record as the most accurate passer in the National Football League's 80-year history. His overall career quarterback rating is 97.6. The rating is based on a statistical formula that averages attempts, yards, completions, interceptions, and touchdowns. Young also has the highest touchdown-interception ratio with 2.22. He holds the NFL record for most consecutive 300-yard games in one season (6). Young has been named to seven consecutive Pro Bowls, and has earned two NFL MVP awards. He played for the San Francisco 49ers and the Tampa Bay Buccaneers.

### PLAYERS WITH THE
### HIGHEST CAREER QUARTERBACK RATING

Lifetime statistical rating

| Steve Young, 1984–2000 | Joe Montana, 1979–1994 | Brett Favre, 1991– | Dan Marino, 1983–2000 | Mark Brunell, 1993– |
|---|---|---|---|---|
| 97.6 | 92.3 | 89.0 | 87.3 | 86.3 |

# Highest Career
# Rushing Total

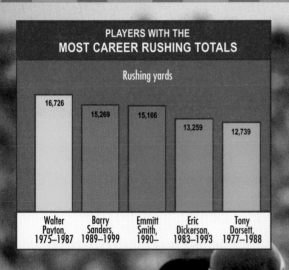

## PLAYERS WITH THE
## MOST CAREER RUSHING TOTALS

Rushing yards

| | 16,726 | 15,269 | 15,166 | 13,259 | 12,739 |
|---|---|---|---|---|---|
| | Walter Payton, 1975–1987 | Barry Sanders, 1989–1999 | Emmitt Smith, 1990– | Eric Dickerson, 1983–1993 | Tony Dorsett, 1977–1988 |

Walter Payton was a first-round draft pick for the Chicago Bears in 1975. He holds the record for all-time rushing yards with 16,726. During his stellar 13-year career with the Bears, Payton set several other records. He holds the record for the most 100-yard rushing games with 77, the most 1,000-yard rushing seasons with 10, the most rushing yards in a single game with 275, and the most career rushing touchdowns with 110. He played in nine Pro Bowls, and was a key part of the Bears' 1985–1986 Super Bowl win. He was inducted into the Football Hall of Fame in 1993.

## Walter Payton

# Most Career Touchdowns

## Jerry Rice

With a career record of 186 touchdowns, Jerry Rice is widely considered to be one of the greatest wide receivers ever to play in the National Football League. He holds a total of 14 NFL records, including career receptions (1,281), receiving yards (19,247), receiving touchdowns (176), consecutive 100-catch seasons (3), most games with 100 receiving yards (64), and many others. He was named NFL Player of the Year twice, *Sports Illustrated* Player of the Year four times, and NFL Offensive Player of the Year once.

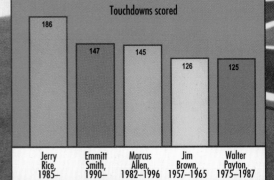

### PLAYERS WITH THE MOST CAREER TOUCHDOWNS

Touchdowns scored

| Jerry Rice, 1985– | Emmitt Smith, 1990– | Marcus Allen, 1982–1996 | Jim Brown, 1957–1965 | Walter Payton, 1975–1987 |
|---|---|---|---|---|
| 186 | 147 | 145 | 126 | 125 |

# Most Single-Season Touchdowns

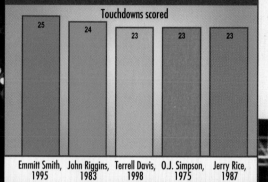

**PLAYERS WITH THE MOST SINGLE-SEASON TOUCHDOWNS**

Touchdowns scored

| Emmitt Smith, 1995 | John Riggins, 1983 | Terrell Davis, 1998 | O.J. Simpson, 1975 | Jerry Rice, 1987 |
|---|---|---|---|---|
| 25 | 24 | 23 | 23 | 23 |

During the 1995 season, the Cowboys' Emmitt Smith scored a record 25 touchdowns. In fact, it only took him 6 seasons to score 100 career touchdowns—the fastest accumulation of touchdowns in National Football League history. Currently in his tenth season, Smith holds four NFL rushing titles and three Super Bowl titles. He also won the Super Bowl XXVIII MVP award. One of the game's most impressive running backs, Smith already has a career total of 12,566 rushing yards. He was the first player in NFL history to have five straight seasons with over 1,400 yards rushing. Smith also leads the NFL with 136 rushing touchdowns.

## Emmitt Smith

241

# Highest Career
## Scoring Total

## Gary Anderson

Gary Anderson is the Minnesota Vikings' top kicker. Altogether he has scored 2,059 points in his 19 seasons of professional play. He also holds several other NFL records, including postseason field goals made, with 28 in his career; field goals made, with 461 in his career; and career postseason scoring, with 143 points. In 1998 Anderson hit 35-of-35 field goals and became the first NFL player to go an entire season without missing a kick. Anderson was first signed by the Pittsburgh Steelers in 1982 and played 13 seasons there. He played two years with the Philadelphia Eagles, one year with the San Francisco 49ers, and then joined the Vikings in 1998.

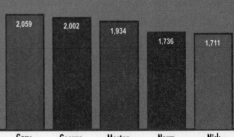

**PLAYERS WITH THE**
**HIGHEST CAREER SCORING TOTAL**

Points scored

| Gary Anderson, 1982– | George Blanda, 1949–1975 | Morten Anderson, 1980– | Norm Johnson, 1983–1999 | Nick Lowery, 1978–1996 |
|---|---|---|---|---|
| 2,059 | 2,002 | 1,934 | 1,736 | 1,711 |

# Team with the Most
# Super Bowl Wins

## Cowboys and 49ers

### TEAMS WITH THE MOST SUPER BOWL WINS

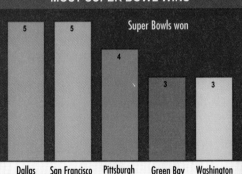

Super Bowls won

| Dallas Cowboys | San Francisco 49ers | Pittsburgh Steelers | Green Bay Packers | Washington Redskins |
|----------------|---------------------|---------------------|-------------------|---------------------|
| 5 | 5 | 4 | 3 | 3 |

To date, the San Francisco 49ers and the Dallas Cowboys have each won a total of five Super Bowl championships. The 49ers had their first win in 1982, and repeated their victory in 1985, 1989, 1990, and 1995. The first championship win for the Cowboys was in 1972, which was followed by wins in 1978, 1993, 1994, and 1996. Out of those 10 victories, the game with the most spectators was Super Bowl XXVII, when Dallas defeated the Buffalo Bills at the Rose Bowl in Pasadena, California in 1993.

*Dallas Cowboys celebrating victory*

# Super Bowl with the
# Highest Attendance

## Super Bowl XIV

Super Bowl XIV took place on January 20, 1980, in front of 103,985 lucky fans who crowded into the Rose Bowl in Pasadena, California. The matchup was between the Pittsburgh Steelers and the Los Angeles Rams. The Steelers won the day with a score of 31–19. The game's Most Valuable Player, Steelers quarterback Terry Bradshaw, set career Super Bowl records for the most touchdowns passed (9), and the most passing yards (932). This was Bradshaw's second consecutive year as the game's Most Valuable Player.

### SUPER BOWLS WITH THE HIGHEST ATTENDANCE

Attendance

| Super Bowl XIV, 1980 | Super Bowl XVII, 1983 | Super Bowl XI, 1977 | Super Bowl XXI, 1987 | Super Bowl VII, 1973 |
|---|---|---|---|---|
| 103,985 | 103,667 | 103,424 | 101,063 | 90,182 |

# Team with the Most
# Stanley Cup Wins

## Montreal Canadiens

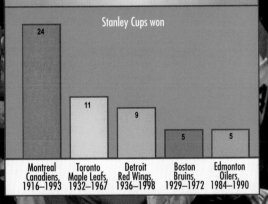

**TEAMS WITH THE MOST STANLEY CUP WINS**

Stanley Cups won

| Montreal Canadiens, 1916–1993 | Toronto Maple Leafs, 1932–1967 | Detroit Red Wings, 1936–1998 | Boston Bruins, 1929–1972 | Edmonton Oilers, 1984–1990 |
|---|---|---|---|---|
| 24 | 11 | 9 | 5 | 5 |

The Montreal Canadiens have won an amazing 24 Stanley Cup victories between 1916 and 1993. That's almost one-quarter of all the Stanley Cups ever played. The Canadiens were created in December of 1909 by J. Ambrose O'Brien to play for the National Hockey Association (NHA). They eventually made the transition into the National Hockey League. Today, they play at Montreal's Molson Center. Over the years, the Canadiens have included such great players as Maurice Richard, George Hainsworth, Jacques Lemaire, and Emile Bouchard.

*Montreal Canadiens with Stanley Cup*

# Most Career Points

# Wayne Gretzky

Many people consider Canadian-born Wayne Gretzky to be the greatest player in the history of the National Hockey League. In fact, he is called the "Great One." During his 20–year career, he scored an unbelievable 2,857 points and 894 goals. In fact, Gretzky was the first person in the NHL to average more than two points per game. He officially retired from the sport in 1999 and was inducted into the Hockey Hall of Fame that same year. After his final game, the NHL retired his jersey number (99).

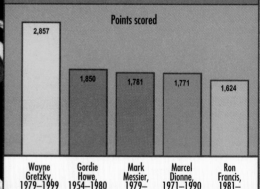

**PLAYERS WHO SCORED THE MOST CAREER POINTS**

Points scored

| Wayne Gretzky, 1979–1999 | Gordie Howe, 1954–1980 | Mark Messier, 1979– | Marcel Dionne, 1971–1990 | Ron Francis, 1981– |
|---|---|---|---|---|
| 2,857 | 1,850 | 1,781 | 1,771 | 1,624 |

# Goalie with the
## Most Career Wins

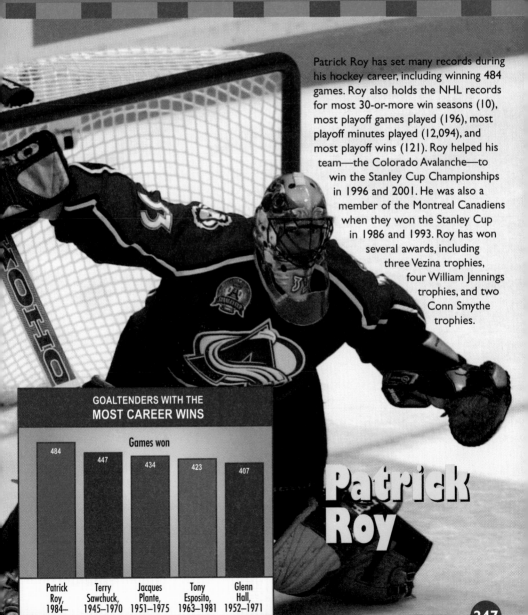

Patrick Roy has set many records during his hockey career, including winning **484** games. Roy also holds the NHL records for most 30-or-more win seasons (10), most playoff games played (196), most playoff minutes played (12,094), and most playoff wins (121). Roy helped his team—the Colorado Avalanche—to win the Stanley Cup Championships in 1996 and 2001. He was also a member of the Montreal Canadiens when they won the Stanley Cup in 1986 and 1993. Roy has won several awards, including three Vezina trophies, four William Jennings trophies, and two Conn Smythe trophies.

**Patrick Roy**

### GOALTENDERS WITH THE MOST CAREER WINS

Games won

| Patrick Roy, 1984– | Terry Sawchuck, 1945–1970 | Jacques Plante, 1951–1975 | Tony Esposito, 1963–1981 | Glenn Hall, 1952–1971 |
|---|---|---|---|---|
| 484 | 447 | 434 | 423 | 407 |

# Most Points in a Single Game

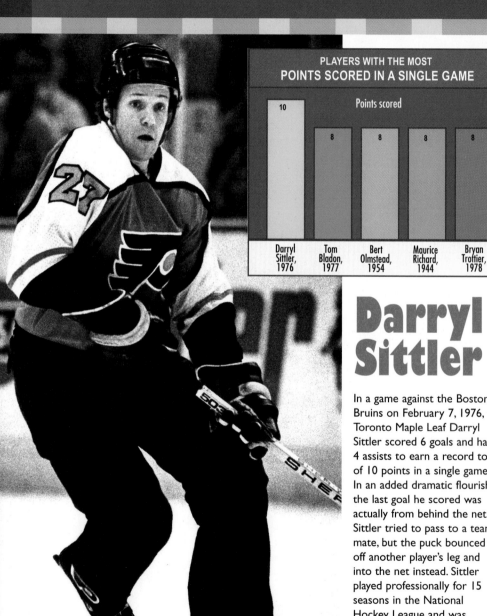

### PLAYERS WITH THE MOST POINTS SCORED IN A SINGLE GAME

Points scored

| Darryl Sittler, 1976 | Tom Bladon, 1977 | Bert Olmstead, 1954 | Maurice Richard, 1944 | Bryan Trottier, 1978 |
|---|---|---|---|---|
| 10 | 8 | 8 | 8 | 8 |

## Darryl Sittler

In a game against the Boston Bruins on February 7, 1976, Toronto Maple Leaf Darryl Sittler scored 6 goals and had 4 assists to earn a record total of 10 points in a single game. In an added dramatic flourish, the last goal he scored was actually from behind the net. Sittler tried to pass to a teammate, but the puck bounced off another player's leg and into the net instead. Sittler played professionally for 15 seasons in the National Hockey League and was inducted into the Hockey Hall of Fame in 1989.

# Most Career
# Hat Tricks

## Wayne Gretzky

During his record-setting career, Wayne Gretzky scored a total of 50 hat tricks (scoring 3 goals in the same game). Born in Brantford, Canada, Gretzky began his professional career in 1978, when he joined the Indianapolis Racers, part of the World Hockey Association (WHA). He moved to the NHL when he was traded to the Edmonton Oilers in 1979. He became team captain and led the Oilers to four Stanley Cup victories. He also won the Art Ross Memorial Trophy 10 times in his career, and was the first player ever to receive the Hart Memorial Trophy.

### PLAYERS WITH THE
### MOST CAREER HAT TRICKS

Hat tricks scored

| | Hat tricks scored |
|---|---|
| Wayne Gretzky, 1979–1999 | 50 |
| Mario Lemieux, 1984–1997, 2000– | 40 |
| Mike Bossy, 1977–1987 | 39 |
| Phil Esposito, 1969–1980 | 32 |

# Man with the Most Major Tournament Wins

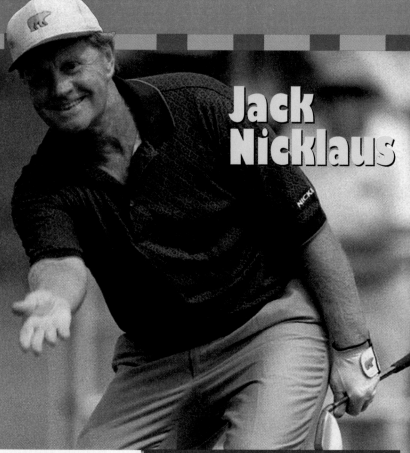

## Jack Nicklaus

After turning professional in 1962, Jack Nicklaus won a total of 18 major championships including 6 Masters, 5 PGAs, 4 U.S. Opens, and 3 British Opens. He was a member of the winning U.S. Ryder Cup team six times, and was an individual World Cup winner a record three times. Nicklaus was also named PGA Player of the Year five times. He was inducted into the World Golf Hall of Fame in 1974, and joined the U.S. Senior PGA Tour in 1990. In addition to playing the game, Nicklaus has designed close to 200 golf courses and written a number of popular books about the sport.

### MEN WITH THE MOST MAJOR TOURNAMENT WINS

Major tournaments won

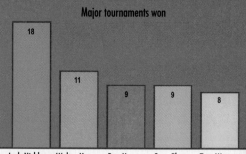

| Jack Nicklaus, 1963–1986 | Walter Hagen, 1914–1929 | Ben Hogan, 1946–1953 | Gary Player, 1959–1978 | Tom Watson, 1975–1983 |
|---|---|---|---|---|
| 18 | 11 | 9 | 9 | 8 |

# Woman with the Most Major Tournament Wins

## Patty Berg

Patty Berg won 16 major tournaments during her 15 years as a professional golfer. After much success as an amateur, she turned professional in 1940 and won her first major tournament in 1943 at the Women's Western Open. She went on to win 57 professional career victories and was the Ladies Professional Golf Association's (LPGA) top money winner three times. She served as president of the LPGA from 1949 to 1952. Berg was inducted into the LPGA Hall of Fame in 1951, the PGA Hall of Fame in 1978, and the International Women's Hall of Fame in 1980.

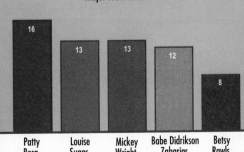

### WOMEN WITH THE MOST MAJOR TOURNAMENT WINS

Major tournaments won

| Patty Berg, 1943–1957 | Louise Suggs, 1948–1961 | Mickey Wright, 1954–1969 | Babe Didrikson Zaharias, 1948–1954 | Betsy Rawls, 1951–1975 |
|---|---|---|---|---|
| 16 | 13 | 13 | 12 | 8 |

# Fastest Man in the
# Boston Marathon

## MEN WITH THE FASTEST BOSTON MARATHON TIME

### Race time in hours/minutes/seconds

| Cosmas Ndeti, 1994 | Moses Tanui, 1998 | Robert de Castella, 1986 | Ibrahim Hussein, 1992 | Gelindo Bordin, 1990 |
|---|---|---|---|---|
| 2:07:15 | 2:07:34 | 2:07:51 | 2:08:14 | 2:08:19 |

In 1994, Cosmas Ndeti completed the Boston Marathon in 2 hours, 7 minutes, and 15 seconds. In this exciting race, Ndeti reached the finish line only four seconds before his closest competitor. A native of Machakos, Kenya, Ndeti had three consecutive Boston Marathon wins from 1993 to 1995. In fact, he is the only man ever to run a time under 2:10:00 in four consecutive Boston Marathons. Amazingly, Ndeti won all of his marathons by negative splitting—running the last half of the race faster than the first.

## Cosmas Ndeti

# Fastest Woman in the Boston Marathon

## Uta Pippig

German runner Uta Pippig set the women's record for the Boston Marathon in 1994 when she finished the race in 2 hours, 21 minutes, and 45 seconds. This record time means she averaged approximately 11 miles (18 km) per hour over the 26.2-mile (42.2-km) course. She also won the contest in 1995 and 1996, and is one of only two women to win the marathon in three consecutive years. During her career, Pippig has also won the New York City Marathon, the Berlin Marathon, and the Leipzig Marathon.

### WOMEN WITH THE FASTEST BOSTON MARATHON TIME

Race time in hours/minutes/seconds

| Uta Pippig, 1994 | Joan Benoit, 1983 | Fatuma Roba, 1998 | Fatuma Roba, 1999 | Olga Markova, 1992 |
|---|---|---|---|---|
| 2:21:45 | 2:22:43 | 2:23:21 | 2:23:25 | 2:23:43 |

# Most Olympic Gold Medals in Men's Basketball

## United States

The United States' men's basketball team has won gold medals in 12 out of the 14 Olympic Games in which they have participated. That means they have an Olympic winning percentage of 86%. In fact, only two other teams have ever won an Olympic gold medal in men's basketball (USSR and Yugoslavia). Basketball was invented in the United States in 1891, but did not become part of the Olympics until the 1936 games in Berlin, Germany. The United States won that very first competition and continued to take the gold for the next six Olympic Games.

### COUNTRIES WITH THE MOST OLYMPIC GOLD MEDALS IN BASKETBALL

Olympic gold medals

| USA | USSR | Yugoslavia |
| --- | --- | --- |
| 12 | 2 | 1 |

Light

# Country with the Most
# Soccer Gold Medals

# Hungary/
# Great Britain

Both Hungary and Great Britain have each won Olympic gold medals in men's soccer a record three times. Soccer was first included in the 1900 and 1904 games on a trial basis, but official Olympic soccer competition began in 1908. Hungary won the competition in 1952, 1964, and 1968. Great Britain triumphed in the 1900, 1908, and 1912 Olympics. In 1920, Great Britain pulled out of the competition to protest professional athletes competing in Olympic soccer, but the country rejoined in 1946. Since then, European teams have dominated the competition, and soccer remains the most popular sport throughout Europe.

*Hungarian soccer player (left) and Israeli soccer player in competition*

### COUNTRIES WITH THE
### MOST GOLD MEDALS IN MEN'S SOCCER

Gold medals won

| Great Britain | Hungary | USSR | Uruguay |
|:---:|:---:|:---:|:---:|
| 3 | 3 | 2 | 2 |

# Country with the Most Men's Volleyball Gold Medals

## U.S.S.R.

From 1964 to 1980, the U.S.S.R. men's volleyball team won the Olympic competition three times. The Soviets, who first competed in the Summer Olympic Games of 1952, have a long Olympic tradition of excelling at team sports. According to old Olympic rules, athletes had to remain amateurs in their sport in order to compete. The Soviet teams kept that status, but were supported by the Sports State Committee as they trained. Although the Soviet Union has broken up, many Russian athletes still excel in volleyball.

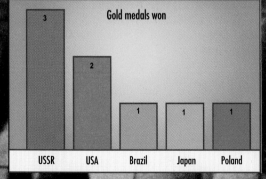

**COUNTRIES WITH THE MOST GOLD MEDALS IN MEN'S VOLLEYBALL**

Gold medals won

| USSR | USA | Brazil | Japan | Poland |
|------|-----|--------|-------|--------|
| 3 | 2 | 1 | 1 | 1 |

# Country with the Most Women's Volleyball Gold Medals

## U.S.S.R.

**COUNTRIES WITH THE MOST GOLD MEDALS IN WOMEN'S VOLLEYBALL**

Gold medals won

| USSR | Cuba | Japan | China |
|------|------|-------|-------|
| 4 | 3 | 2 | 1 |

The Soviet women's volleyball team has won a total of four Olympic competitions. They received gold medals in 1968, 1972, 1980, and 1988. Volleyball, which was invented in America in 1895 by William Morgan, became very popular in the Soviet Union. In fact, at the 1952 World Championships in Moscow, a whopping 40,000 fans attended each match. The first men's and women's official Olympic volleyball competitions were held in Tokyo, Japan, during the 1964 Olympic Games.

257

# Most Men's Gold Medals in
# Cross-Country Skiing

## Björn Daehlie

Björn Daehlie, a Norwegian cross-country skier with the nickname "Rocketman," has won eight gold medals in his event. He also holds the records for the most Winter Olympic medals won, and most Winter gold medals won. Daehlie won a career total of 12 Olympic medals from 1992 to 1998. He earned gold medals twice in the combined pursuit, the 10-kilometer (6.2-mile) race, 50-kilometer (31-mile) race, and the 410-kilometer (254.7-mile) race relay. Daehlie also won 14 World Championship gold medals and 6 overall World Cup titles.

### MEN WITH THE MOST GOLD MEDALS IN CROSS-COUNTRY SKIING

Gold medals won

| Björn Daehlie, Norway | Sixten Jernberg, Sweden | Gunde Svan, Sweden | Thomas Wassberg, Sweden | Nikolai Zimyatov, USSR |
|---|---|---|---|---|
| 8 | 4 | 4 | 4 | 4 |

# Most Women's Gold Medals in
# Cross-Country Skiing

Russian cross-country skier Lyubov Yegorova has won six gold medals. She won her first three gold medals, as well as two silver medals, during the 1992 Winter Olympics in Albertville, France. She later earned another three gold medals and one silver in Lillehammer during the 1994 Winter Olympics. In fact, Yegorova was one of the two top medal winners at the Winter Games in Lillehammer. She also won ten World Cup events between 1991 and 1994, including the World Cup title in 1993.

## Lyubov Yegorova

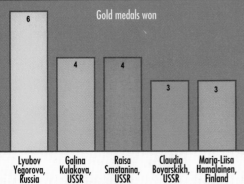

**WOMEN WITH THE MOST GOLD MEDALS IN CROSS-COUNTRY SKIING**

Gold medals won

| Lyubov Yegorova, Russia | Galina Kulakova, USSR | Raisa Smetanina, USSR | Claudia Boyarskikh, USSR | Marja-Liisa Hamalainen, Finland |
|---|---|---|---|---|
| 6 | 4 | 4 | 3 | 3 |

# Man with the Most Figure Skating Gold Medals

## Gillis Grafstrom

Gillis Grafstrom, an artistic figure skater from Sweden, won three Olympic gold medals and one silver medal during his career. He also competed for, and won, the Men's World Figure Skating Championship title a total of three times. Grafstrom developed several daring and innovative moves during his career, including the flying sit-spin. Later in his career, he coached Norwegian skater Sonja Henie to three Olympic gold medals, which propelled her into the international spotlight as a major star in world ice-skating.

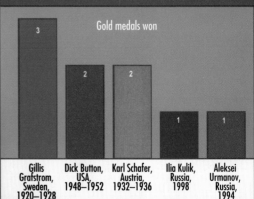

**MEN WITH THE MOST GOLD MEDALS IN FIGURE SKATING**

Gold medals won

| Gillis Grafstrom, Sweden, 1920–1928 | Dick Button, USA, 1948–1952 | Karl Schafer, Austria, 1932–1936 | Ilia Kulik, Russia, 1998 | Aleksei Urmanov, Russia, 1994 |
|---|---|---|---|---|
| 3 | 2 | 2 | 1 | 1 |

# Woman with the Most Figure Skating Gold Medals

## Sonja Henie

During the Winter Olympic Games of 1928, 1932, and 1936, Sonja Henie won three gold medals. She won her first medal at just 15 years of age. Classical ballet training allowed Henie to create artistic routines that were very popular with the audiences. After turning professional in 1936, she became the star of the Hollywood Ice Revues, which toured throughout America and Europe. Henie was also a popular actress who made 10 motion pictures. When she passed away in 1969, she was one of the wealthiest women in the world.

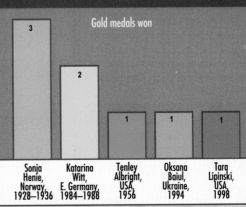

**WOMEN WITH THE MOST GOLD MEDALS IN FIGURE SKATING**

Gold medals won

| Sonja Henie, Norway, 1928–1936 | Katarina Witt, E. Germany, 1984–1988 | Tenley Albright, USA, 1956 | Oksana Baiul, Ukraine, 1994 | Tara Lipinski, USA, 1998 |
|---|---|---|---|---|
| 3 | 2 | 1 | 1 | 1 |

# Most Men's Gold Medals in Track and Field

*Carl Lewis*

## Carl Lewis / Paavo Nurmi

Both Carl Lewis and Paavo Nurmi have won nine track-and-field gold medals. Lewis, however, had the most wins in consecutive Olympics. Lewis won his first four gold medals in 1984 at the Los Angeles games. He later won two medals in Seoul, Korea, two more gold medals in Barcelona, Spain, and one medal in Atlanta, Georgia.

Paavo Nurmi set many Olympic records in his career, including the fastest 1,500 and 5,000 meter dash. He also held the record for the farthest distance run in an hour—11 miles, 1,648 yards (19,210 m).

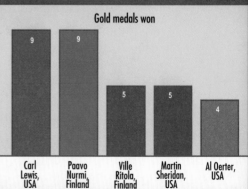

**MEN WITH THE MOST GOLD MEDALS IN TRACK AND FIELD**

Gold medals won

| Carl Lewis, USA | Paavo Nurmi, Finland | Ville Ritola, Finland | Martin Sheridan, USA | Al Oerter, USA |
|---|---|---|---|---|
| 9 | 9 | 5 | 5 | 4 |

# Most Women's Gold Medals in Track and Field

## Evelyn Ashford, Fanny Blankers-Koen, Betty Cuthbert, and Bärbel Eckert Wockel

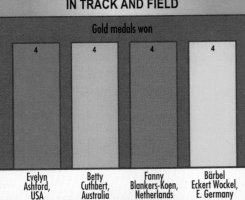

### WOMEN WITH THE MOST GOLD MEDALS IN TRACK AND FIELD

Gold medals won

| Evelyn Ashford, USA | Betty Cuthbert, Australia | Fanny Blankers-Koen, Netherlands | Bärbel Eckert Wockel, E. Germany |
|---|---|---|---|
| 4 | 4 | 4 | 4 |

Evelyn Ashford, Betty Cuthbert, Fanny Blankers-Koen, and Bärbel Eckert Wockel each won four gold medals in various Olympic track-and-field events. Betty Cuthbert—an Australian sprinter—won three of her medals during the 1956 Summer Olympics in Melbourne, Australia, and one at the Olympics in Tokyo. American sprinter Evelyn Ashford is the oldest woman to win an Olympic gold in track and field at age 35. Fanny Blankers-Koen was the first woman to win four gold medals at one Olympics. Bärbel Eckert Wockel ran in the 200-meter dash and relay races in the 1976 and 1980 Olympics.

*Betty Cuthbert*

# Top Career
# Gold Medal Winners

*Mark Spitz*

## Larissa Latynina, Carl Lewis, Paavo Nurmi, Mark Spitz

Larisa Latynina, Carl Lewis, Paavo Nurmi, and Mark Spitz each won nine gold medals during their Olympic careers. Lewis, a track-and-field superstar, won his medals in consecutive games between 1984 and 1996. Latynina, a gymnast in the 1950s and 1960s, is the only woman to win nine gold medals. Between 1920 and 1928, Nurmi collected his gold medals and set several track-and-field records in the process. Swimmer Mark Spitz swam his way to nine gold medals in the 1968 and 1972 games.

**OLYMPIC ATHLETES WITH THE**
**MOST CAREER GOLD MEDALS**

Lifetime gold medals

| Larissa Latynina, USSR | Carl Lewis, USA | Paavo Nurmi, Finland | Mark Spitz, USA | Bjorn Daehlie, Norway |
|---|---|---|---|---|
| 9 | 9 | 9 | 9 | 8 |

# Most
# Olympic Medals

# Larissa Latynina

Soviet gymnast Larissa Latynina won an amazing 18 medals between 1956 and 1964. During that time, she competed in the Olympic Games at Melbourne, Australia; Rome, Italy; and Tokyo, Japan. In addition to her record-setting nine gold medals, she also won five silver and four bronze medals. Latynina—who studied at the Kiev State Institute of Physical Culture—became a national gymnastic coach after retiring from Olympic competition. She also helped to plan the 1980 Moscow Olympics, which were held in her home country.

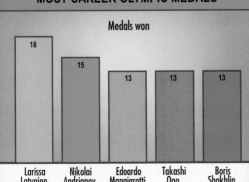

## ATHLETES WITH THE MOST CAREER OLYMPIC MEDALS

Medals won

| | | | | |
|---|---|---|---|---|
| 18 | 15 | 13 | 13 | 13 |
| Larissa Latynina, Soviet Union Gymnastics | Nikolai Andrianov, USSR Gymnastics | Edoardo Mangiarotti, Italy Fencing | Takashi Ono, Japan Gymnastics | Boris Shakhlin, USSR Gymnastics |

# Most Men's Gold Medals in
# Gymnastics

Japanese gymnast Kato Sawao won eight Olympic gold medals from 1968 to 1976. He picked up his first three golds in Mexico City during the 1968 Summer Games, where he won for combined exercises, floor exercises, and team competition. Four years later, in Munich, Germany, Sawao won the gold in the parallel bars, and again in the combined exercises and team competition. Sawao earned his last two gold medals in Montreal, Canada, for his second consecutive win on the parallel bars and the Japanese team's fifth consecutive overall win.

# Kato Sawao

**MEN WITH THE MOST GOLD MEDALS IN GYMNASTICS**

Gold medals won

| Kato Sawao, Japan | Nikolai Andrianov, USSR | Viktor Chukarin, USSR | Boris Shakhlin, USSR | Akinori Nakayama, Japan |
|---|---|---|---|---|
| 8 | 7 | 7 | 7 | 6 |

# Most Women's Gold Medals in Gymnastics

## Larissa Latynina

Larissa Latynina, one of the Soviet Union's greatest gymnasts, won nine gold medals during her Olympic career—the first woman ever to accomplish this. She earned her first three individual medals during the 1956 Olympic Games in Melbourne, Australia, winning the combined exercises, the vault, and the floor exercises. Four years later, in Rome, Italy, Latynina picked up her next two individual golds with repeat wins in the combined and floor exercises. She later won the gold medal for floor exercises in Tokyo, Japan, in 1964. Latynina also won a gold medal with the Soviet gymnastic team in each of her three Olympics.

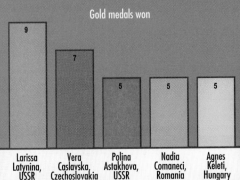

**WOMEN WITH THE MOST GOLD MEDALS IN GYMNASTICS**

Gold medals won

| Larissa Latynina, USSR | Vera Caslayska, Czechoslovakia | Polina Astakhova, USSR | Nadia Comaneci, Romania | Agnes Keleti, Hungary |
|---|---|---|---|---|
| 9 | 7 | 5 | 5 | 5 |

# Most Men's Gold Medals in
# Swimming

## Mark Spitz

Mark Spitz, a swimmer from the United States, won nine gold medals during the Olympic Games in Mexico City and Munich, Germany. He was also the first athlete to win seven medals during one Olympics. Although Spitz boasted that he would win six medals in 1968, he in fact only won two. But later, in 1972, Spitz not only won all four of the individual competitions he entered, he also set world records in each. That same year, he picked up three other golds as a member of several men's relay teams.

### MEN WITH THE MOST GOLD MEDALS IN SWIMMING

Gold medals won

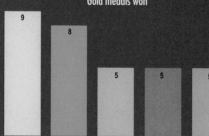

| Mark Spitz, USA | Matt Biondi, USA | Charles Daniels, USA | Tom Jager, USA | Don Schollander, USA |
|-----------------|------------------|----------------------|----------------|----------------------|
| 9 | 8 | 5 | 5 | 5 |

# Most Women's Gold Medals in
# Swimming

## Jenny Thompson

Jenny Thompson swam her way into the record books when she won three gold medals in the 2000 Olympic Games in Sydney, Australia. Thompson, who already had five gold medals from the 1992 and 1996 games, has earned all of her medals in relay events. She has a silver and a bronze from individual competitions. Thompson is the only U.S. woman to win eight career gold medals. She is also one of only two women to ever win three gold medals in the same event. She has won three gold medals each in the 4x100 free and 4x200 free relay events. During her swimming career, which began at age 8, Thompson has won 23 national titles and 26 NCAA championships.

**WOMEN WITH THE MOST GOLD MEDALS IN SWIMMING**

Gold medals won

| Jenny Thompson, USA | Kristin Otto, E. Germany | Krisztina Egerszegi, Hungary | Janet Evans, USA | Kornelia Ender, E. Germany |
|---|---|---|---|---|
| 8 | 6 | 5 | 5 | 4 |

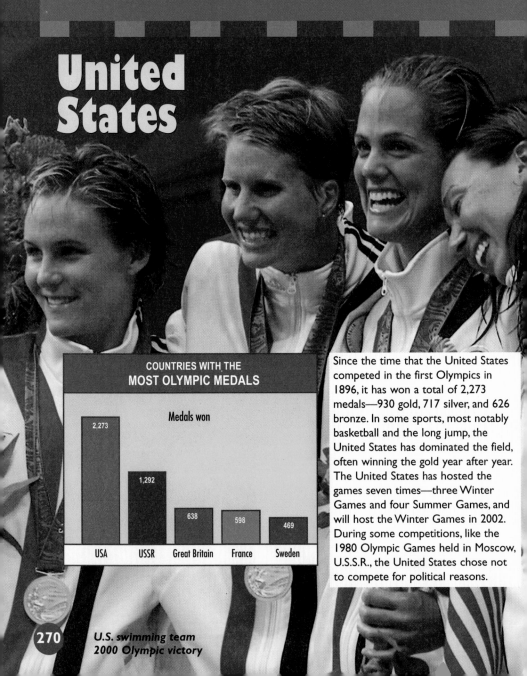

# Country with the Most Medals

## United States

### COUNTRIES WITH THE MOST OLYMPIC MEDALS

Medals won

| Country | Medals |
|---|---|
| USA | 2,273 |
| USSR | 1,292 |
| Great Britain | 638 |
| France | 598 |
| Sweden | 469 |

Since the time that the United States competed in the first Olympics in 1896, it has won a total of 2,273 medals—930 gold, 717 silver, and 626 bronze. In some sports, most notably basketball and the long jump, the United States has dominated the field, often winning the gold year after year. The United States has hosted the games seven times—three Winter Games and four Summer Games, and will host the Winter Games in 2002. During some competitions, like the 1980 Olympic Games held in Moscow, U.S.S.R., the United States chose not to compete for political reasons.

U.S. swimming team
2000 Olympic victory

# Man with the Most
# World Cup Goals

## Gerd Müller

Gerd Müller, a striker for West Germany, scored a total of 14 goals in the 1970 and 1974 World Cups. During his impressive soccer career, Müller competed in many other international championships and earned several awards. In 1970, he was the European Championship Top Scorer, and was later part of the winning European Championship team in 1972. Müller also received the Golden Boot Award (European Top Scorer) in 1970 and 1972, and the European Footballer of the Year Award in 1970.

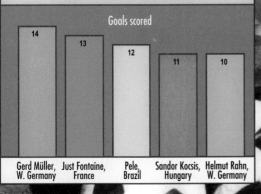

**MEN WITH THE
MOST WORLD CUP GOALS**

Goals scored

| Gerd Müller, W. Germany | Just Fontaine, France | Pele, Brazil | Sandor Kocsis, Hungary | Helmut Rahn, W. Germany |
|---|---|---|---|---|
| 14 | 13 | 12 | 11 | 10 |

# Country with the Most World Cup Points

## Brazil / Germany

Both Brazil and Germany have each accumulated 26 points in World Cup championships. (A win is worth four points, runner up is worth three points, third place is worth two points, and fourth place is worth one point.) The World Cup was organized by the Fédération Internationale de Football Association (FIFA). The international competition was first played in 1930. Both professional and amateur players are allowed to compete. In Brazil, soccer is both the national sport and the national pastime. Many Brazilian superstar players are even considered national heroes.

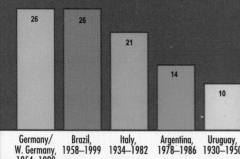

### COUNTRIES WITH THE MOST WORLD CUP POINTS

| Germany/ W. Germany, 1954–1990 | Brazil, 1958–1999 | Italy, 1934–1982 | Argentina, 1978–1986 | Uruguay, 1930–1950 |
|---|---|---|---|---|
| 26 | 26 | 21 | 14 | 10 |

*Brazilian soccer team*

# Top Country in Women's Soccer

The United States' women's soccer team became the highest-ranked team in the world when they won the Women's World Cup in July of 1999. By adding three points from the win to their lifetime score, the U.S. pulled ahead of Norway. The team set some other records during that championship as well. An amazing 90,185 tickets were sold for the final match between the United States and China—a world's record for any women's sporting event. For all the games in the entire championship, some 650,000 tickets were sold, resulting in $23 million in revenue.

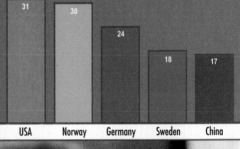

**HIGHEST-RANKING WOMEN'S SOCCER TEAMS IN WOMEN'S WORLD CUP**

Total points

| USA | Norway | Germany | Sweden | China |
|-----|--------|---------|--------|-------|
| 31  | 30     | 24      | 18     | 17    |

## United States

*Soccer match between the United States (in white) and China*

273

# Man with the Most Singles
# Grand Slam Titles

## Pete Sampras

Pete Sampras holds the title for the most grand slam male singles titles with 13 victories. He has won two Australian Opens, seven Wimbledon titles, and four U.S. Opens between 1990 and 2000. Sampras, who is still a top competing player, finished number one in the world for the sixth straight year in 1998. He has won more than $39 million in prize money as of 1999.

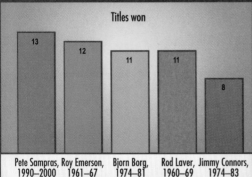

**MEN WITH THE MOST**
**SINGLES GRAND SLAM TITLES**

Titles won

| | | | | |
|---|---|---|---|---|
| 13 | 12 | 11 | 11 | 8 |
| Pete Sampras, 1990–2000 | Roy Emerson, 1961–67 | Bjorn Borg, 1974–81 | Rod Laver, 1960–69 | Jimmy Connors, 1974–83 |

# Woman with the Most Singles
## Grand Slam Titles

**WOMEN WITH THE MOST
SINGLES GRAND SLAM TITLES**

Titles won

| Margaret Court Smith, 1960–1975 | Steffi Graf, 1987–1996 | Helen Wills-Moody, 1923–1938 | Chris Evert-Lloyd, 1974–1986 | Martina Navratilova, 1974–1995 |
|---|---|---|---|---|
| 24 | 22 | 19 | 18 | 18 |

Margaret Court Smith won 24 grand slam singles titles between 1960 and 1975. She was only the second woman to win the French, British, U.S., and Australian titles in the same year. She is the only woman ever to win all four titles during one year in both the singles and doubles competitions. During her amazing career, she won a total of 66 Grand Slam championships—more than any other woman. Court was the world's top-seeded female player from 1962–1965, 1969–1970, and 1973. She was inducted into the International Tennis Hall of Fame in 1979.

# Margaret Court Smith

# Popular Culture Records

**Art • Music • Awards & Prizes • Books & Newspapers
Television • Movies • Fashion • Theater**

# World's Most Expensive Painting By a Woman Artist

# The Conversation

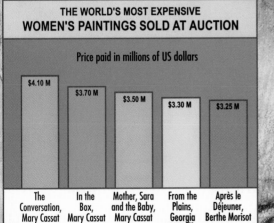

**THE WORLD'S MOST EXPENSIVE
WOMEN'S PAINTINGS SOLD AT AUCTION**

Price paid in millions of US dollars

| The Conversation, Mary Cassatt | In the Box, Mary Cassat | Mother, Sara and the Baby, Mary Cassatt | From the Plains, Georgia O'Keeffe | Après le Déjeuner, Berthe Morisot |
|---|---|---|---|---|
| $4.10 M | $3.70 M | $3.50 M | $3.30 M | $3.25 M |

On May 11, 1988, Mary Cassatt's oil painting *The Conversation* sold for $4.1 million at a Christie's auction and is now part of a private collection. Cassatt studied at the Pennsylvania Academy of Fine Arts before studying art in Europe in 1865. After settling in Paris, she began to work with acclaimed Impressionists Edouard Manet and Edgar Degas. Cassatt was greatly influenced by both their subjects and their techniques. The majority of her paintings and pastel sketches feature women and children participating in everyday activities.

# Most Valuable Auctioned Painting

# Portrait of Dr. Gachet

The *Portrait of Dr. Gachet*, an oil painting by Dutch Impressionist Vincent van Gogh, was sold to Ryoei Saito at a Christie's auction in 1990 for $75 million. This was not the first time that van Gogh's work brought such a high price—three of the five most expensive paintings ever auctioned were van Gogh's. Dr. Gachet lived from 1828 to 1909 and specialized in homeopathy. The doctor loved the arts and supported several famous artists. In May of 1890, Gachet invited van Gogh to stay with him at Auvers-sur-Oise in France. There, van Gogh painted 70 canvases in just 70 days.

**THE WORLD'S MOST VALUABLE**
**PAINTINGS SOLD AT AUCTION**

Price in millions of US dollars

| Painting | Price |
|---|---|
| Portrait of Dr. Gachet, van Gogh | $75 M |
| Au Moulin de la Galette, Pierre-Auguste Renoir | $71 M |
| Portrait de l'Artiste Sans Barbe, van Gogh | $65 M |
| Les Noces de Pierrette, Pablo Picasso | $51.6 M |
| Irises, van Gogh | $49 M |

# World's
# Best-selling Album

Michael Jackson's smash hit *Thriller* was first released on March 16, 1982. Within only a few weeks, it had become one of the most popular albums of all time—both nationally and internationally. To date, it has sold approximately 40 million copies. *Thriller* was released on the Epic record label and was produced by mastermind Quincy Jones. The album received eight Grammy® Awards and contained six top-ten singles. *Thriller* featured many pop singles, including "Beat It," "Billie Jean," and "Wanna Be Startin' Somethin.'"

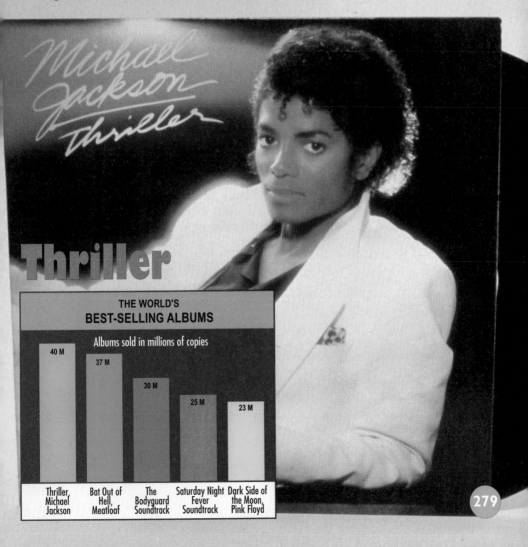

**Thriller**

### THE WORLD'S
### BEST-SELLING ALBUMS

Albums sold in millions of copies

| Thriller, Michael Jackson | Bat Out of Hell, Meatloaf | The Bodyguard Soundtrack | Saturday Night Fever Soundtrack | Dark Side of the Moon, Pink Floyd |
|---|---|---|---|---|
| 40 M | 37 M | 30 M | 25 M | 23 M |

# World's Best-Selling Male
# Recording Artist

## Garth Brooks

Country superstar Garth Brooks has sold more than 101 million copies of his recordings since his career took off in 1989. His first album, titled *Garth Brooks*, reached the fourth slot on the country charts. *No Fences* was released a year later and featured the hit singles "The Thunder Rolls" and "Friends in Low Places." Brooks' third album—Grammy-winning *Ropin' the Wind*—became the first album in history to debut at number one on both the pop and country charts. Some of Brooks' other best-selling albums include *Sevens* (1997) and *Garth Brooks In…The Life of Chris Gaines* (1999).

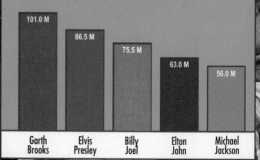

**THE WORLD'S BEST-SELLING MALE RECORDING ARTISTS**

Certified units sold, in millions

| Garth Brooks | Elvis Presley | Billy Joel | Elton John | Michael Jackson |
|---|---|---|---|---|
| 101.0 M | 86.5 M | 75.5 M | 63.0 M | 56.0 M |

# World's Best-Selling Female
# Recording Artist

# Barbra Streisand

During her 39 years as a singer, Barbra Streisand has sold more than 66 million copies of her work. She has recorded more than 50 albums, and has more gold albums than any other entertainer in history. Some of her recordings include *People*, *Color Me Barbra*, *Emotion*, and *Higher Ground*. Streisand received a Lifetime Achievement Award at the Grammys® in 1995. She has also directed, produced, and appeared in many movies. Some of her best-known film work includes roles in *Funny Girl*, *The Way We Were*, *Yentl*, and *The Prince of Tides*.

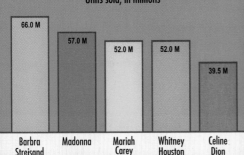

**THE WORLD'S BEST-SELLING FEMALE RECORDING ARTISTS**

Units sold, in millions

| Barbra Streisand | Madonna | Mariah Carey | Whitney Houston | Celine Dion |
|---|---|---|---|---|
| 66.0 M | 57.0 M | 52.0 M | 52.0 M | 39.5 M |

# World's Best-Selling Recording Group

## The Beatles

Since their first official recording session in September 1962, the Beatles have sold more than 163 million copies of their music. In fact, when "Beatlemania" hit the United States in 1964, the album *Meet the Beatles* sold more than one million copies in just two weeks. In the two years that followed, they had 26 top-40 singles. The "Fab Four," as they were called, were John Lennon, Paul McCartney, George Harrison, and Ringo Starr. Together they recorded many albums now considered to be rock masterpieces, such as *Rubber Soul*, *Sgt. Pepper's Lonely Hearts Club Band*, and *The White Album*. The group broke up in 1969. In 2001, however, their newly released greatest hits album—*The Beatles I*—reached the top of the charts.

### THE WORLD'S BEST-SELLING RECORDING GROUP

Millions of copies sold

| Group | Millions of copies sold |
|-------|-------------------------|
| The Beatles | 163.5 M |
| Led Zeppelin | 100.5 M |
| Pink Floyd | 68.5 M |
| Eagles | 66.5 M |
| AC/DC | 63.0 M |

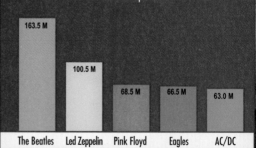

From left: *George Harrison, John Lennon, Ringo Starr, Paul McCartney*

# Artist with the Most Grammy®
# Nominations

## Quincy Jones

Quincy Jones has been nominated for a record 77 Grammy® Awards. He has won an astounding 26 Grammys®, the second highest total of all time. He has written songs for many music legends, including Duke Ellington, Count Basie, and Ray Charles. He has also written 33 major motion picture scores, and the theme songs for television shows such as *Sanford and Son* and *The Bill Cosby Show*. Jones was also the producer for Michael Jackson's *Thriller*, the world's best-selling album. Jones has also received one Emmy and seven Academy Award nominations.

### THE ARTISTS WITH THE MOST GRAMMY® NOMINATIONS

Grammy® nominations

| Quincy Jones | Sir Georg Solti | Stevie Wonder | Pierre Boulez | Vladimir Horowitz |
|---|---|---|---|---|
| 77 | 73 | 62 | 56 | 45 |

# Man with the Most
# Grammy® Awards

## Sir Georg Solti

Sir Georg Solti earned 31 Grammy® Awards during his distinguished music career. He debuted as a concert pianist in the Budapest Orchestra, but soon became its conductor. He went on to serve as musical director of the Bavarian State Opera, the Frankfurt City Opera, and the Royal Opera House. He was knighted by Queen Elizabeth II in 1972 for his great contributions to music. Solti also received many prestigious awards from around the world, including Germany's Knight Commander's Cross and Great Britain's Gold Medal of the Royal Philharmonic.

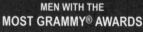

### MEN WITH THE MOST GRAMMY® AWARDS

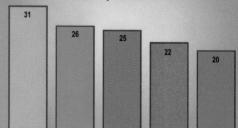

Grammy® awards won

| Sir Georg Solti, Hungary | Quincy Jones, USA | Vladimir Horowitz, Russia | Pierre Boulez, France | Henry Mancini, USA |
|---|---|---|---|---|
| 31 | 26 | 25 | 22 | 20 |

# Woman with the Most
# Grammy® Nominations

## Aretha Franklin

This undisputed queen of rhythm-and-blues music has received an amazing 39 Grammy® nominations and won a record total of 15 Grammy® Awards. Eleven of her Grammys® came for Best R&B Vocal Performance, two for Best Soul Gospel Performance, and one for Best R&B Performance by a Duo with George Michael. Some of her most famous recordings include "Respect," "I Never," "Natural Woman," and "Who's Zoomin' Who?" In 1985, Franklin became the first woman in history to be inducted into the Rock 'n Roll Hall of Fame.

### WOMEN WITH THE MOST GRAMMY® NOMINATIONS

Grammy® nominations

| Aretha Franklin | Linda Ronstadt | Ella Fitzgerald | Shirley Caesar | Alison Krauss |
|---|---|---|---|---|
| 39 | 25 | 20 | 20 | 16 |

# Most
# Nobel Peace Prizes

## International Red Cross

The International Committee of the Red Cross was founded in 1863 by Jean-Henri Dunant. Since its creation, it has been honored with three Nobel Peace Prizes. The International Red Cross is a non-governmental organization with world headquarters in Geneva, Switzerland. It is directed by15–25 members, all of whom are Swiss. The members meet 10 times a year to refresh the organization's commitment to help war victims and to ensure that humanitarian actions are observed throughout the world.

### THE WORLD'S RECIPIENTS OF THE NOBEL PEACE PRIZE

Nobel Peace prizes won

| International Red Cross | Office of the UN High Commissioner of Refugees | Amnesty International | United Nations Children's Fund |
|---|---|---|---|
| 3 | 2 | 1 | 1 |

# Most Journalism
# Pulitzer Prizes

# St. Louis Post-Dispatch

The *St. Louis Post-Dispatch*—the main morning newspaper in St. Louis, Missouri—has won five Pulitzer Prizes for Journalism. Joseph Pulitzer himself founded this paper in 1878, by combining the *St. Louis Dispatch* with the *St. Louis Post*. The paper was dedicated to honest reporting and broke several large stories. The paper's high-quality writing and journalism ethics brought in an impressive 22,000 subscribers in just three years. To improve their international reporting, the Post-Dispatch began sending journalists around the world to cover breaking stories in 1906—a fairly new practice at the time.

## NEWSPAPERS WITH THE MOST PULITZER PRIZE WINS

Pulitzer Prizes won

| Newspaper | Prizes |
| --- | --- |
| St. Louis Post-Dispatch | 5 |
| Los Angeles Times | 4 |
| New York World | 4 |
| New York Times | 3 |
| New York Newsday | 3 |

# The All-time
# Best-selling Book

## The Bible

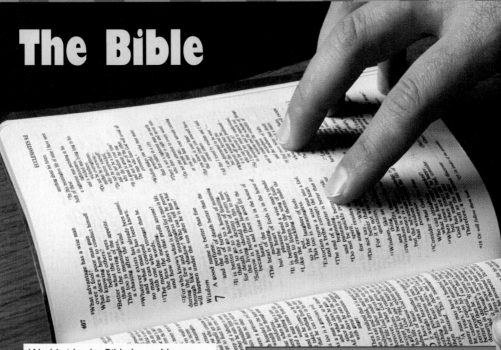

Worldwide, the Bible has sold more than six billion copies. That is enough copies to give each person in the world one book! In fact, the Bible has sold more copies than the top 20 all-time bestselling books combined! The Bible is the sacred scripture of both Judaism and Christianity, although each religion includes different information in its holy book. The book has been sold in such large numbers partly because its followers make up two of the top six religions in the world. There are approximately 1.8 billion Christians and 18 million Jews in the world today.

**THE WORLD'S BEST-SELLING BOOKS**

Number of copies sold in billions and millions

| The Bible | Quotations from Mao Tse-Tung | American Spelling Book | The Guinness Book of Records | The Pokey Little Puppy |
|---|---|---|---|---|
| 6 B | 800 M | 100 M | 81 M | 17 M |

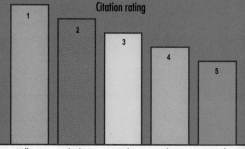

# World's
# Most-Cited Author

Although it would be nearly impossible to get an exact number of citations for a certain author, *Citations*—a widely used U.S. library database—registers more than 15,500 books by and about William Shakespeare. His brilliant and unique style of writing relates to many different cultures. Born in Stratford-upon-Avon in England in the mid-1500s, Shakespeare wrote his plays for small theaters. Most of those plays are still studied in schools and colleges of all kinds around the world. There have also been dozens of movies made from his plays or about his life.

## William Shakespeare

### AUTHORS WHO ARE
### MOST FREQUENTLY CITED

Citation rating

| 1 | 2 | 3 | 4 | 5 |
|---|---|---|---|---|
| William Shakespeare | Charles Dickens | Sir Walter Scott | Johann Goethe | Aristotle |

# Newspaper with the Highest Circulation

## Yomiuri Shimbun

讀賣新聞

THE YOMIURI SHIMBUN

第44662号　(日刊)©読売新聞社2000年

短期0.25％

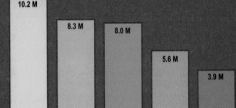

**NEWSPAPERS WITH THE HIGHEST DAILY CIRCULATION**

Average daily circulation in millions

| Yomiuri Shimbun, Japan | Asahi Shimbun, Japan | Sichuan Ribao, China | Bild, Germany | Mainichi Shimbun, Japan |
|---|---|---|---|---|
| 10.2 M | 8.3 M | 8.0 M | 5.6 M | 3.9 M |

The *Yomiuri Shimbun* is Japan's largest newspaper. It sells an average of 10.2 million copies each day, but is read by roughly twice that number. Each paper is read by approximately two people, which means that the *Yomiuri Shimbun* is read by about 22% of the entire country. This daily paper has both morning and evening editions, and many Japanese buy both each day. Like North American newspapers, its sections include politics, economy, crime, society, and sports. The *Daily Yomiuri On-Line*, the newspaper's Web site, also offers its articles on the Internet.

政府の延期請求否決

ゼロ金利政策の変更について会見する速水日銀総裁（11日午後7時、日銀で）＝竹田津敦史撮影

# Country that Spends the Most on Books

**Norway**

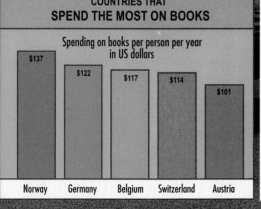

### COUNTRIES THAT SPEND THE MOST ON BOOKS

Spending on books per person per year in US dollars

| | | | | |
|---|---|---|---|---|
| $137 | $122 | $117 | $114 | $101 |
| Norway | Germany | Belgium | Switzerland | Austria |

Norwegians like to read. Norway is the top book-buying country in the world, with the average person spending about $137 a year on books. The country has a population of 4,503,440 people who altogether spend a total of more than $613 million on books. Reading is the main indoor activity in Norway. Norwegians read more books than any other population in the world. More than 80% of the people read at least one book a year and about 38% read more than 20 books a year.

# World's Highest-Earning Author

Suspense writer Stephen King earned about $44 million in 2000. King was a high school English teacher in 1974 when he sold *Carrie*, his first novel. The book, and later the movie version, were very successful, and King soon became a household name. Some of his more than 40 novels include *Salem's Lot*, *The Shining*, *Firestarter*, *Misery*, and *The Green Mile*. King was also the screenwriter for several movies based on his books, such as *Creepshow*, *Pet Sematary*, *Needful Things*, and *Thinner*.

## THE WORLD'S HIGHEST-EARNING AUTHORS

2000 earnings in millions of US dollars

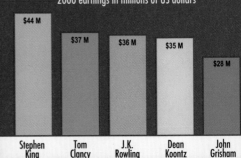

| Stephen King | Tom Clancy | J.K. Rowling | Dean Koontz | John Grisham |
|---|---|---|---|---|
| $44 M | $37 M | $36 M | $35 M | $28 M |

## Stephen King

# Most Popular
# Television Show

# Who Wants to Be a Millionaire

## MOST POPULAR TELEVISION SHOWS

### Percentage of TV households watching, 2000

| Who Wants to Be a Millionaire Tuesday | Who Wants to Be a Millionaire Thursday | Who Wants to Be a Millionaire Sunday | ER | Friends |
|---|---|---|---|---|
| 18.6% | 17.5% | 17.1% | 16.9% | 14.0% |

*Who Wants to Be a Millionaire*, a trivia-based quiz show hosted by Regis Philbin, was the most popular television show in 2000. It was seen, on average, by more than 18% of the American television viewing audience on Tuesday nights. On the show, a contestant answers a series of questions as he or she works up to the million-dollar question. If a contestant gets stumped, he or she can phone a friend, ask the audience, or delete two of the possible multiple-choice answers. This type of show isn't only popular in the U.S. There are 40 versions of the show that air in 56 countries.

# Most-Watched Television
# Episode

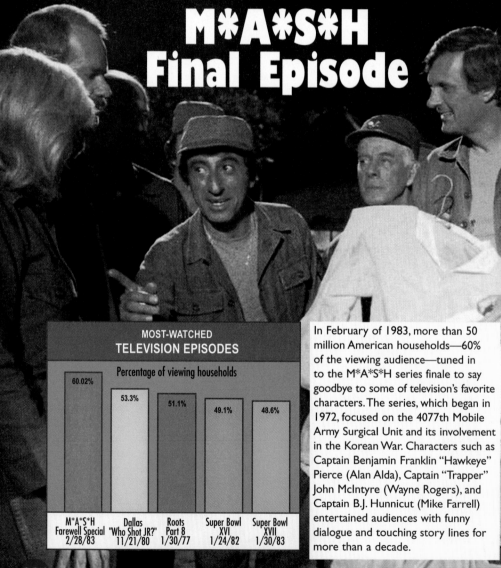

## M*A*S*H
## Final Episode

### MOST-WATCHED
### TELEVISION EPISODES

**Percentage of viewing households**

| M*A*S*H Farewell Special 2/28/83 | Dallas "Who Shot JR?" 11/21/80 | Roots Part 8 1/30/77 | Super Bowl XVI 1/24/82 | Super Bowl XVII 1/30/83 |
|---|---|---|---|---|
| 60.02% | 53.3% | 51.1% | 49.1% | 48.6% |

In February of 1983, more than 50 million American households—60% of the viewing audience—tuned in to the M*A*S*H series finale to say goodbye to some of television's favorite characters. The series, which began in 1972, focused on the 4077th Mobile Army Surgical Unit and its involvement in the Korean War. Characters such as Captain Benjamin Franklin "Hawkeye" Pierce (Alan Alda), Captain "Trapper" John McIntyre (Wayne Rogers), and Captain B.J. Hunnicut (Mike Farrell) entertained audiences with funny dialogue and touching story lines for more than a decade.

# Longest-Running
# Prime-Time Series

# Wonderful
# World of Disney

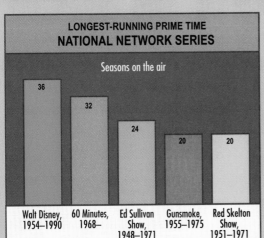

**LONGEST-RUNNING PRIME TIME
NATIONAL NETWORK SERIES**

Seasons on the air

| | | | | |
|---|---|---|---|---|
| 36 | 32 | 24 | 20 | 20 |
| Walt Disney, 1954–1990 | 60 Minutes, 1968– | Ed Sullivan Show, 1948–1971 | Gunsmoke, 1955–1975 | Red Skelton Show, 1951–1971 |

Walt Disney's first regularly scheduled series began on the ABC Television Network in October of 1954. Disney wanted to provide some of the same magic and entertainment that families had enjoyed at his movies. Through the years, as the series switched networks, its name changed several times. Some of the series names included "Disneyland," "Walt Disney Presents," and "The Wonderful World of Disney." During its 36 years on the air, the show has only had 2 hosts: Walt Disney himself, and later, Walt Disney Co. CEO Michael Eisner.

**295**

# World's Highest-Earning
# Talk Show Host

## Oprah Winfrey

Oprah Winfrey—the second-highest earning entertainer on the 2001 Forbes Celebrity 100 list—reportedly grossed $150 million in 2000. She is the first woman to own and produce her own talk show—part of Harpo Productions (Harpo is Oprah spelled backwards). One of Oprah's newest ventures is launching a magazine titled O. She was inducted into the National Women's Hall of Fame in 1999.

### THE HIGHEST-EARNING TALK SHOW HOSTS

2000 earnings in millions of US dollars

| Oprah Winfrey | Regis Philbin | Rosie O'Donnell | David Letterman | Jay Leno |
|---|---|---|---|---|
| $150 M | $35 M | $25 M | $20 M | $17 M |

# TV Show with the Most Consecutive Emmy® Wins

## Frasier

*Frasier*—the hilarious comedy about a Seattle radio talk show host—has won five consecutive Emmy® Awards in the Outstanding Comedy Series category. Between 1994–1998, *Frasier* has earned a total of 21 Emmys® for comedy, including 3 for best lead actor and 3 for best supporting actor. Kelsey Grammer, who plays the title character, has been nominated 9 times for his portrayal of the same character on three different television shows—*Cheers, Wings,* and *Frasier.* The show has also won the Peabody Award, Golden Globe Awards, the TV Guide Award, and many others.

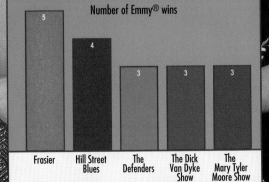

**SHOWS WITH THE MOST CONSECUTIVE EMMY® WINS**

Number of Emmy® wins

| Frasier | Hill Street Blues | The Defenders | The Dick Van Dyke Show | The Mary Tyler Moore Show |
|---|---|---|---|---|
| 5 | 4 | 3 | 3 | 3 |

# World's Highest-Paid Actor

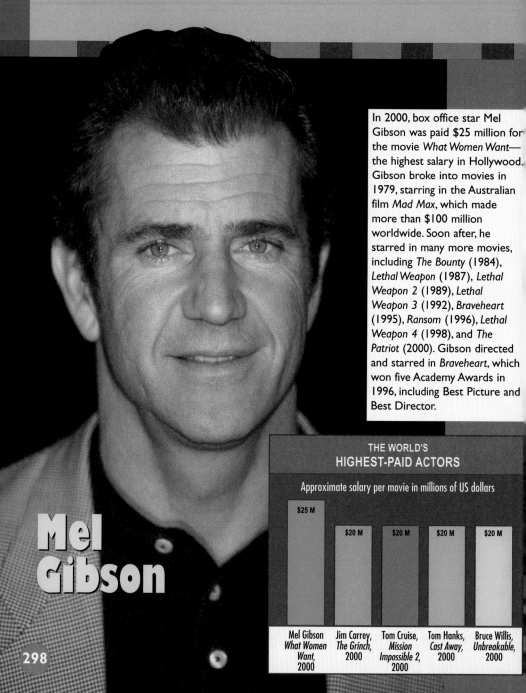

In 2000, box office star Mel Gibson was paid $25 million for the movie *What Women Want*—the highest salary in Hollywood. Gibson broke into movies in 1979, starring in the Australian film *Mad Max*, which made more than $100 million worldwide. Soon after, he starred in many more movies, including *The Bounty* (1984), *Lethal Weapon* (1987), *Lethal Weapon 2* (1989), *Lethal Weapon 3* (1992), *Braveheart* (1995), *Ransom* (1996), *Lethal Weapon 4* (1998), and *The Patriot* (2000). Gibson directed and starred in *Braveheart*, which won five Academy Awards in 1996, including Best Picture and Best Director.

## Mel Gibson

### THE WORLD'S HIGHEST-PAID ACTORS

Approximate salary per movie in millions of US dollars

| $25 M | $20 M | $20 M | $20 M | $20 M |
|---|---|---|---|---|
| Mel Gibson *What Women Want,* 2000 | Jim Carrey, *The Grinch,* 2000 | Tom Cruise, *Mission Impossible 2,* 2000 | Tom Hanks, *Cast Away,* 2000 | Bruce Willis, *Unbreakable,* 2000 |

# World's Highest-Paid Actress

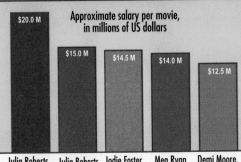

## Julia Roberts

**THE WORLD'S HIGHEST-PAID ACTRESSES**

Approximate salary per movie, in millions of US dollars

| $20.0 M | $15.0 M | $14.5 M | $14.0 M | $12.5 M |
|---|---|---|---|---|
| Julia Roberts, *Erin Brockovich,* 2000 | Julia Roberts, *The Runaway Bride,* 1999 | Jodie Foster, *Anna and the King,* 1999 | Meg Ryan, *You've Got Mail,* 1998 | Demi Moore, *StripTease,* 1996 |

American superstar Julia Roberts was paid a record-breaking $20 million to portray a working single mom in the 2000 box office hit *Erin Brockovich*, which won her an Academy Award for Best Actress. Roberts made her professional debut in 1988 on the television show "Crime Story," and went on to impress movie critics in the film *Mystic Pizza*, released later that same year. She has also received Oscar® nominations for her roles in *Steel Magnolias* and *Pretty Woman*. Some of Roberts's other well-known movies include *The Pelican Brief*, *My Best Friend's Wedding*, *Notting Hill*, and *Runaway Bride*.

299

# World's Top Grossing Movie

## Titanic

Directed by James Cameron in 1998, *Titanic* has grossed more than $600 million in the United States and more than $1.8 billion worldwide—and that's in just two years. This action-packed drama/romance is set aboard the White Star Line's lavish *RMS Titanic,* the largest moving object ever built, in 1912. The two main characters, wealthy Rose DeWitt Bukater and the poor immigrant, Jack Dawson—played by Kate Winslet and Leonardo DiCaprio—meet, fall in love, and are separated as the *Titanic* sinks into the North Atlantic on the morning of April 15, 1912.

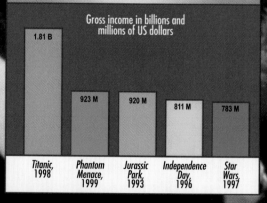

**THE WORLD'S HIGHEST-GROSSING MOVIES**

Gross income in billions and millions of US dollars

| | | | | |
|---|---|---|---|---|
| 1.81 B | 923 M | 920 M | 811 M | 783 M |
| Titanic, 1998 | Phantom Menace, 1999 | Jurassic Park, 1993 | Independence Day, 1996 | Star Wars, 1997 |

# World's Top-Grossing Kid's Movie

## Snow White and the Seven Dwarfs

Snow White and the Seven Dwarfs, a Walt Disney production that debuted in 1937, has earned an amazing $1.03 billion in box office receipts to date. (To compare the success of films throughout the decades, it is necessary to adjust for inflation.) Snow White and the Seven Dwarfs was the first animated feature film ever, and it cost $1.4 million to make. More than 750 artists were used during the three-year production. Many of the songs in the movie, including "Some Day My Prince Will Come," and "Whistle While You Work," have become

### THE WORLD'S TOP-GROSSING KID'S MOVIES

Box office receipts in billions and millions of constant dollars

| | | | | |
|---|---|---|---|---|
| $1.03 B | $812 M | $725 M | $656 M | $646 M |
| Snow White and the Seven Dwarfs | Star Wars | E.T. The Extra-Terrestrial | 101 Dalmatians | Bambi |

# World's Top Grossing
# Movie Musical

## Grease

Grease debuted in 1978 and earned more than $340 million in box office receipts. It has remained such a popular movie with audiences of all ages that it was re-released in theaters for its twentieth anniversary. Before it was adapted for film, it was one of Broadway's biggest hits. Today, more than two decades after its original release, Grease is still one of the top 10 video purchases. It has also sold more than 20 million double-soundtrack albums. Some of the soundtrack's songs are performed by the two main stars of the movie—John Travolta and Olivia Newton-John.

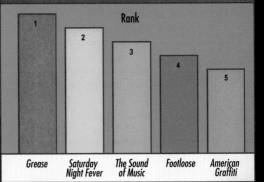

### THE WORLD'S TOP-GROSSING MOVIE MUSICALS

Rank

| Grease | Saturday Night Fever | The Sound of Music | Footloose | American Graffiti |
| 1 | 2 | 3 | 4 | 5 |

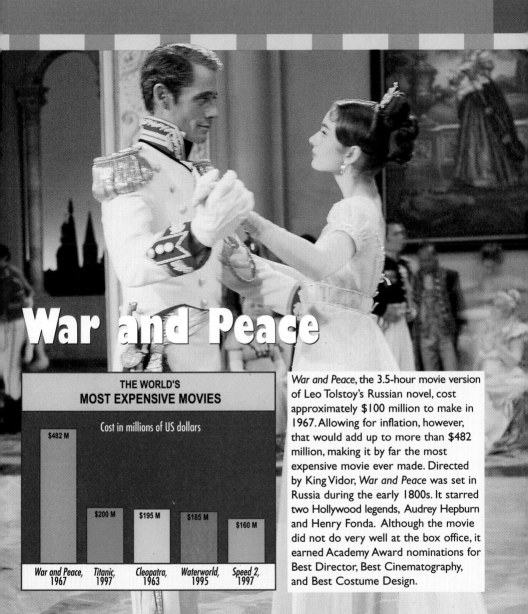

# World's Most
# Expensive Movie

# War and Peace

## THE WORLD'S MOST EXPENSIVE MOVIES

Cost in millions of US dollars

|  |  |
|---|---|
| War and Peace, 1967 | $482 M |
| Titanic, 1997 | $200 M |
| Cleopatra, 1963 | $195 M |
| Waterworld, 1995 | $185 M |
| Speed 2, 1997 | $160 M |

*War and Peace*, the 3.5-hour movie version of Leo Tolstoy's Russian novel, cost approximately $100 million to make in 1967. Allowing for inflation, however, that would add up to more than $482 million, making it by far the most expensive movie ever made. Directed by King Vidor, *War and Peace* was set in Russia during the early 1800s. It starred two Hollywood legends, Audrey Hepburn and Henry Fonda. Although the movie did not do very well at the box office, it earned Academy Award nominations for Best Director, Best Cinematography, and Best Costume Design.

# Movie with the Most
# Oscar® Nominations

## All About Eve / Titanic

All About Eve and Titanic both received a record-setting 14 Academy Award nominations. Out of those nominations, All About Eve won 6 Oscars® and Titanic won 11. All About Eve was a dark, psychological drama that starred Bette Davis as Margo Channing, an aging Broadway star who becomes friends with a seemingly shy fan, Eve Harrington (played by Anne Baxter). As it turns out, Harrington is actually after Channing's fame and success. Titanic is the historically-based epic of two young people who are tragically separated in one of the worst maritime disasters in history.

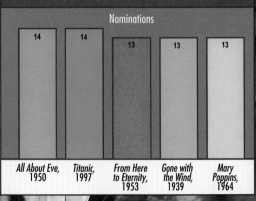

**MOVIES WITH THE MOST OSCAR® NOMINATIONS**

Nominations

| Movie | Nominations |
|-------|-------------|
| All About Eve, 1950 | 14 |
| Titanic, 1997 | 14 |
| From Here to Eternity, 1953 | 13 |
| Gone with the Wind, 1939 | 13 |
| Mary Poppins, 1964 | 13 |

# Movie with the Most Oscars®

**MOVIES WITH THE MOST OSCAR® WINS**

Oscars® won

| Ben-Hur, 1959 | Titanic, 1997 | West Side Story, 1961 | Gigi, 1958 | The Last Emperor, 1987 |
|---|---|---|---|---|
| 11 | 11 | 10 | 9 | 9 |

# Ben-Hur / Titanic

*Ben-Hur* and *Titanic* are the only two films in Hollywood history to win 11 Academy Awards. *Ben-Hur*, which was released in 1959, is a Biblical epic based on an 1880 novel by General Lee Wallace. Its $15 million production cost made *Ben-Hur* the most expensive film of its time. Charlton Heston, who played the hero, won the only Oscar® of his career for this movie. Some other Oscars® included Best Picture, Best Supporting Actor (Hugh Griffith), and Best Score. Some of *Titanic's* wins included Best Picture and Best Director (James Cameron).

*Ben-Hur*

# World's Oldest Oscar® Winner

## Jessica Tandy

In 1989, Jessica Tandy won an Academy Award for her starring role in *Driving Miss Daisy*, which she made when she was 80 years old. In addition to the Best Actress award, the movie also earned an Oscar® for Best Picture. The comedy/drama was about race relations in the South from 1948 to 1973, and co-starred Morgan Freeman. Tandy was born in London in 1909 and became a U.S. citizen in 1954. During her 67-year acting career she won three Tony Awards and appeared in many well-known films, including *The Birds*, *Cocoon*, and *Fried Green Tomatoes*.

### THE WORLD'S OLDEST OSCAR® WINNERS

Age at win

| Jessica Tandy, 1989 | Melvin Douglas, 1979 | Don Ameche, 1985 | Dame Peggy Ashcroft, 1984 | John Gielgud, 1981 |
|---|---|---|---|---|
| 80 | 79 | 77 | 77 | 77 |

# World's Youngest Oscar® Winner

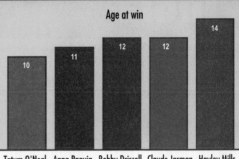

## THE WORLD'S YOUNGEST OSCAR® RECIPIENTS

### Age at win

| Tatum O'Neal, 1973 | Anna Paquin, 1993 | Bobby Driscoll, 1949 | Claude Jarman, 1946 | Hayley Mills, 1960 |
|---|---|---|---|---|
| 10 | 11 | 12 | 12 | 14 |

Tatum O'Neal won her first and only Academy Award in 1973, when she was only 10 years old. Although younger children had won special Oscars®, she is the youngest person to win the award in a competition against adults. Her Best Supporting Actress Award was for her portrayal of Addie in *Paper Moon*, which also starred her father, Ryan O'Neal. The movie told the story of a con-man and his daughter during the Depression of the 1930s. O'Neal also won a Golden Globe for this role. Subsequent Tatum O'Neal movies include *Little Darlings*, *International Velvet*, and *The Bad News Bears*.

## Tatum O'Neal

# Country That Makes the Most Movies

## India

During the 1990s, filmmakers in India produced an average of 851 movies per year. With that availability, it's not surprising that movies have replaced theater as the favorite national pastime of India. But many Indian movies also enjoy a worldwide audience. Brilliant moviemakers such as Satyajit Ray have brought India's film industry international recognition. In fact, Bombay (Mumbai) has earned the nickname "Bollywood," for its Hollywood-like productions. One famous Bollywood actress is Madhuri Dixit, who starred in *Hum Aapke Hain Koun*, which grossed $63 million in 1994.

### COUNTRIES THAT PRODUCE THE MOST MOVIES

Average number of movies produced each year

|  |  |
|---------|--------|
| India | 851 |
| USA | 569 |
| Japan | 252 |
| Russia | 192 |
| France | 143 |

# Country with the Most Moviegoers

China

TITANIC
泰坦尼克号

## COUNTRIES WITH THE MOST MOVIEGOERS

Annual movie attendance
in billions and millions

| China | India | USA | Russia | Japan |
|-------|-------|-----|--------|-------|
| 14.4 B | 4.2 B | 981 M | 140 M | 130 M |

According to the most recent statistics available, approximately 14.4 billion movie tickets were sold in China in 1997. That's enough to give everyone in China three tickets and every other person in the world two tickets! China also creates about 140 films each year, ranking sixth in world movie production. The Chinese enjoy many of the same kinds of movies that are popular with Western audiences. One recent film is *Suzhou River*, a winner at the 2000 Hong Kong International Film Festival. Some Chinese-language films such as *Crouching Tiger, Hidden Dragon* are seen by audiences around the world.

309

# World's Highest-Earning
# Supermodel

## Claudia Schiffer

This native-born German model earned $9 million in 2000. She has been on the covers of more than 500 magazines, including *Vogue, Harper's Bazaar, Elle,* and *Cosmopolitan*. She was also the first model to appear on the cover of *Rolling Stone*. After being discovered in a German disco in 1987, Schiffer began modeling for such clothing companies as Guess?, Chanel, Versace, Ralph Lauren, and Valentino. She also has several advertising contracts, including deals with Pepsi and L'Oreal. Schiffer enjoys acting, and has appeared in several movies.

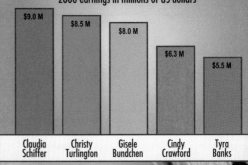

**SOME OF THE WORLD'S HIGHEST-EARNING SUPERMODELS**

2000 earnings in millions of US dollars

| Claudia Schiffer | Christy Turlington | Gisele Bundchen | Cindy Crawford | Tyra Banks |
|---|---|---|---|---|
| $9.0 M | $8.5 M | $8.0 M | $6.3 M | $5.5 M |

# Longest-Running
# Broadway Show

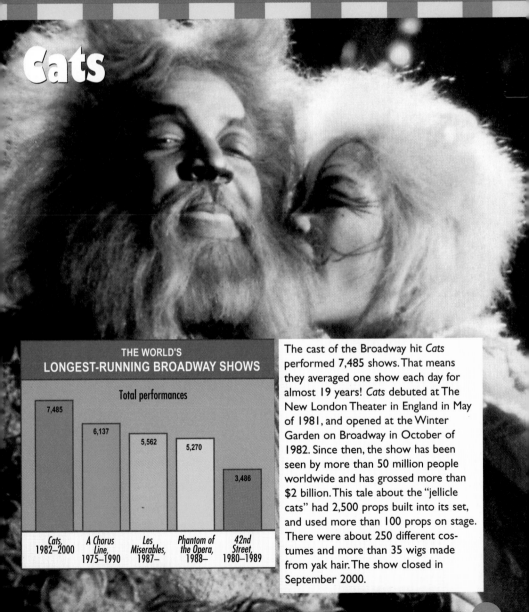

## Cats

### THE WORLD'S
### LONGEST-RUNNING BROADWAY SHOWS

Total performances

| | | | | |
|---|---|---|---|---|
| 7,485 | 6,137 | 5,562 | 5,270 | 3,486 |
| Cats, 1982–2000 | A Chorus Line, 1975–1990 | Les Miserables, 1987– | Phantom of the Opera, 1988– | 42nd Street, 1980–1989 |

The cast of the Broadway hit *Cats* performed 7,485 shows. That means they averaged one show each day for almost 19 years! *Cats* debuted at The New London Theater in England in May of 1981, and opened at the Winter Garden on Broadway in October of 1982. Since then, the show has been seen by more than 50 million people worldwide and has grossed more than $2 billion. This tale about the "jellicle cats" had 2,500 props built into its set, and used more than 100 props on stage. There were about 250 different costumes and more than 35 wigs made from yak hair. The show closed in September 2000.

# Index